HOW TO WIN

X

FACTOR

KEELEY BOLGER

OMNIBUS PRESS

LONDON / NEW YORK / PARIS / SYDNEY / COPENHAGEN / BERLIN / MADRID / TOKYO

D0198042

Copyright © 2009 Omnibus Press
(A Division of Music Sales Limited)

Cover and book designed by Fresh Lemon
Picture research by Jacqui Black & Sarah Bacon

ISBN: 978.1.84938.059.1
Order No: OP53064

Exclusive Distributors
Music Sales Limited,
14/15 Berners Street,
London, W1T 3LJ.

Music Sales Corporation,
257 Park Avenue South,
New York, NY 10010, USA.

Macmillan Distribution Services,
56 Parkwest Drive
Derrimut, Vic 3030,
Australia.

Every effort has been made to trace the copyright holders of the
photographs in this book but one or two were unreachable. We would
be grateful if the photographers concerned would contact us.

Printed by: Gutenberg Press Ltd, Malta

A catalogue record for this book is available from the British Library.

Visit Omnibus Press on the web at www.omnibuspress.com

CONTENTS

ACKNOWLEDGEMENTS

I would like to say a big thank you to Bruno MacDonald, Chris Charlesworth and Zoë Street Howe who've all helped in their separate but equally helpful ways in getting this book on the road. Thanks are also due to Elaine and Adrian Bolger for their continued love and support and especially to Joe Minihane who makes everything possible.

Finally, a huge thanks to all the *X Factor* contestants for being such great sports and for providing us with great entertainment over the last five years.

Keeley Bolger, May 2009

HOW TO WIN X FACTOR

INTRODUCTION

The X Factor has only been on the box for five years but already it tempts 10 million of us to forego doing "things" on a Saturday night so we can sit in and watch it instead. It has made superstars out of humble Hackney girl Leona Lewis, Mancunian chappie Shayne Ward, Beyoncé's biggest fan Alexandra Burke, not to mention making superduperstars out of Simon Cowell, Louis Walsh, Dannii Minogue and Cheryl Cole.

But for every Leona, Shayne or Alexandra, there are 10, maybe 20, Chicos, Steve Brooksteins and, erm, all those other ones.

Despite the probability of sustainable success being very low, thankfully the desire to audition hasn't diminished, with last year's total reported to stand at a whopping

182,000 auditions. But what can a poor singer do, besides holding a note, to improve their chances of impressing the judges and us at home, and scooping the crown?

Get a sharp new look? Romp with one of the camera people or speak in a broad accent? Or is it something else?

Well, let's find out.

HOW TO WIN X FACTOR

chapter one

A BRIEF HISTORY OF TV TALENT SHOWS

"I mean that most sincerely, folks."

It's hard to imagine a world without Simon Cowell's big stamp all over it, but unbelievably most of us hadn't heard of the millionaire mogul even just 10 years ago. How *did* we cope? In fact, just a decade ago, the idea of having a few faded popstars and some curmudgeonly music executives cutting karaoke singers down to size on the telly sounded very odd indeed. Fancy that.

But indeed, just as we had taken fly-on-the-wall reality telly to heart, so we did TV talent shows (with a dash of reality thrown in for good measure). Soon, before we knew it, must-watch TV was charting shameful Scotsman Darius Danesh's unlikely progress on *Popstars* with judge "nasty" Nigel Lythgoe wagging his finger at his bewildering Britney Spears impersonations and putting him in his place. And it wasn't long before the then little-known disparaging dream-maker Simon Cowell whiffed the sweet smell of lucrative TV success, thought he might like some of that too and took over the talent show reins.

So without further ado, here's a brief history of the genre's evolution:

1950s

Canadian Carroll Levis brings over a new TV format from the states – the talent show. Starting off with a radio talent show in the Thirties, Levis eventually lands his own slot on BBC – *The Carroll Levis Discovery Show* – which seeks to find gifted young singers up and down the UK. Believe it or not future Beatles John, Paul and George auditioned with The Quarrymen for Levis in Manchester in 1959 but had to catch the last bus home so never knew whether they'd won or not.

1956

Opportunity Knocks, which started as a radio show, has a first run on the box with Londoner turned Canadian citizen Hughie "I mean that most sincerely folks" Green as the host. The ITV show was different from other talent shows in that the public decided the winner by postal vote and the studio audience showed their reaction to the song with a clap-o-meter (claps recorded were just folly as they weren't cast towards the final tally). The show was then taken over by Thames TV for 12 years and was the first programme to use the telephone vote to decide the winner. The show is later revived by the Beeb in 1987 by Bob Monkhouse and again in the Nineties by Les Dawson.

1968

Welsh folk singer Mary Hopkin wins *Opportunity Knocks* and becomes one of the first artists to secure a contract with The Beatles' own Apple label, thanks to model Twiggy telling her friend Paul McCartney about her. Paul becomes Mary's mentor, producing her debut single, 'Those Were The Days', which goes to number one in the charts.

1973

Derek Hobson presents brand spanking new ITV show *New Faces* to find the latest singing sensation. Judges Tony Hatch and Alan Freeman are lauded for their "mean" scoring (and a young Simon Cowell studiously takes notes). Illustrious contestants include panto favourites The Chuckle Brothers, Roy Walker, Showaddywaddy, Peter Andre and Lenny Henry. The programme is revived by former winner Marti Caine in the Eighties with her catchphrase "press your buttons now" being verbally bandied around the country for the next decade.

1982

Saturday morning kids' show *Saturday Superstore* hosts its 'Search For A Superstar' strand, which sees cocky kids vying for the coveted children's crown. Future Stone Roses keyboardist Nigel Ipinson-Fleming wins the 1987 title with his band Juvenile Jazz. Suck on that Ian Brown.

1986

A very young future Take Thatter Gary Barlow enters the Beeb's annual *Carol Competition,* which was a contest for choir boys and girls up and down the country to perform on TV. Suck on that Robbie Williams.

2000

The nation tunes into ITV every Saturday to hear the future Hear'Say and Liberty X warble The Mamas And The Papas' 'Monday Monday' in the toilets of the *Popstars* studios and see Darius Danesh make bold claims about his future success. The TV talent show is reborn.

2001

Simon Cowell makes his judging debut on telly! The blunt talent-spotter joins "Dr" Neil Fox, Nicki Chapman and Pete Waterman for *Pop Idol, a* spin-off of *Popstars. Pop Idol* was conceived to find the world's next great solo performer. Will Young beats stuttering teen Gareth Gates and eventually lands a role in *Mrs Henderson Presents* with Dame Judi Dench.

2002

Future *X Factor* judge Cheryl Cole is selected to be one of *Popstars: The Rivals* band Girls Aloud, to be managed by judge Louis Walsh. Boy band One True Voice take the male title and are managed by Louis' rival judge, Pete Waterman, but despite initial success, the band split six months after forming on the show. No one's sure what Girls Aloud are up to these days either.

2002

The BBC brings out *Fame Academy* to compete with ITV's *Pop Idol.* The show places an emphasis on training its "students" to write their own songs and escape the "manufactured" label. Current pop star Lemar is probably the show's best-thought-of contestant, with former winners David Sneddon and Alex Parks fading out of the initial limelight shone on them.

2004

Simon Cowell introduces the UK to *The X Factor*, a show that he has recently acquired the rights to, and soon the nation has a hot date with the box every Saturday for the last three months of the year. The popular show comes under fire from *Pop Idol's* Simon Fuller, who managed Spice Girls, who accuses t'other Simon of copying his show *Popstars*. The two reach an out of court settlement and the rest is history.

2006

The BBC starts a search for the next Maria Von Trapp, *How Do You Solve A Problem Like Maria?,* for the West End production of *The Sound Of Music*. Subsequent series include *Any Dream Will Do, I'd Do Anything.*

Et voila.

chapter two

MAKING A GOOD IMPRESSION AT THE AUDITION

"This is my dream. I've wanted this since I was a little girl/boy."

Most people will tell you that their favourite part of the whole *X Factor* is the auditions. Weeks of unadulterated pleasure! The conceited, the talented, the odd, the desperate and those who were told to go by their mums all warble 'Without Wings', to be greeted by a chorus of dismissive sniggers or open mouths from the panellists, while we at home spend 90 minutes of our Saturday engaged in high-volume shouting at the screen.

Even the most talented singer can slip up by being too cocksure, too shy, too normal or too boring. Why, even eventual 2008 winner Alexandra Burke didn't do enough for the judges first time around and was kicked out at Boot Camp. So what hope have the rest of them? Not much it seems.

"We want to feel sorry for contestants on The X Factor,*"*
says psychotherapist and author Phillip Hodson.
*"We know that a lot of them are making fools of themselves
for our entertainment and we're not sure, if we were in the
same place, we wouldn't do the same.*

*"Everyone wants his or her five minutes of fame. The
culture of words, literature, and arts has gone away and
nowadays it's images and pictures. Everyday people have
been given power – and everyday people who watch* The X
Factor *want to see that, and see people like them get their
five minutes' worth. The barriers have come down."*

So, what can be done – besides, you know, singing all
right – to win over the hard-to-please panel? Well, there's
your voice, for one thing. That's speaking voice.

"It's a good idea not to have an accent," says Hodson.
*"Because if you're from the north you'll say things
differently from those in the south. And if you're from the
south you'll say things differently from people in the north.*

*"So try a modern estuary demotic [i.e. talking like Victoria
Beckham, one of* The X Factor's *spiritual godmothers].
You want to sound accessible and modern and as much
like everybody else – and your core audience – as possible.*

"For The X Factor, *you should probably use shorter, simple
sentences. And use popular culture references and clichés,
because people can easily latch onto them and they won't
feel alienated or like you're being snobby.*

"You have to be able to have a different way of speaking to different people. Try to adapt and speak their language."

So when poor Rhydian Roberts bounded into the audition room in 2007, all confidence and amusing puns, it was like he'd just come from outer space in a package labelled "arrogant". What did the poor operatic mite do? One sentence: *"I'm Rhyd or The Rhyddler."* Sorry, what was that? The Rhyddler? The. Rhyddler. Funny as it might have been, our panel's sensitive ears didn't want to hear excessive zaniness – they'd dealt with that all day – and the overly familiar nickname was a bit much.

But the resilient Rhyddler fought back to win the judges' respect. He was told to sing his love ditty – later called *"the worst song I've ever heard"* by Simon Cowell – to a scorn-faced Dannii. Nonetheless, Rhydian kept good face and managed to get through both that song – and, on Simon's request, 'Dancing Queen' – with his eventual mentor, Dannii, pulling faces and rolling her eyes at him.

Rhydian was bumped through to the next round – remarkable, given that he also made some big boo-boos before he even trilled to Cowell and Co. *"Make no bones about it,"* he said before he went into his audition. *"I want to be successful."*

It might be true and we might not like fakers in our *X Factor*, but someone who is ambitious on the telly? Right in front of us as we settle down? In our homes? Nope, we're just here to watch the crazies audition at this stage, not watch *Apprentice* wannabes ("I'm in it to win it",

"I'll give it 110%"). No, we thought at the time. No, "The Rhyddler". We don't buy into your nicknames. Get out.

So where did Rhydian go wrong where 2008 contestant Diana Vickers went right? Well, with her cloud of blonde hair and beaming face, the Lancashire lass soon won over the judges. Before she even opened her mouth, she looked likeable. Pretty but not too up herself and oh-so-bang-on in the *X Factor* tick list.

Take her to-camera piece. Diana dropped several *X Factor* must-says in the space of 30 seconds. *"I love singing, it's my passion."* Kerching. *"I just want to sing in front of people."* Kerrr-ching. *"This is my dream."* KER-CHING. Bonus points for pulling her arms over her chest and looking oh-so-genuine when she said it. Game, set, and match to the 6th former from Accrington.

And, when she went in, she didn't overwhelm the judges with confidence. Because confidence at this stage is a Very Bad Thing. Quiet confidence is a different matter. We're all for that. They can know they're talented but they don't need to tell us that: *we're* ones who want to realise their talent and discover them – albeit in front of the box on a Saturday evening.

So what else can you do to win over the panel? Here are some pointers to bear in mind:

★ Over use the sentence, "This is my dream." Cheryl once had a dream to sing. So did Dannii. Use it, use it, use it.

★ Smile coyly at the judges à la Diana Vickers. You want to look slightly in awe of the judges and all their collected experience and wisdom, but not too much. No one likes a suck-up. Body language expert Leil Lowndes explains: "If you're auditioning before the judges on *The X Factor,* the most important thing to do is not to act too awestruck. Act like an equal. Don't tell them they did well in so and so a show. They'll think, 'Are you to judge?' Instead, tell them how much pleasure, insight or whatever their work has given you. And thank them."

★ Develop a minor speech impediment. You're probably best to go for a lisp at this stage as it's easier to pull off than anything more serious. Then you can show off the singing talent that, extraordinarily, isn't tainted by your lisp. Plus, if you get through at this stage, you'll have more time to work on the big hitters: stammers and stutters (which they may interpret as nerves and be more patient with your performance).

★ Create some sort of drama and sense that you nearly missed out on the audition. That way, we'll all feel relieved that you miraculously managed to make it despite being almost being mown down on your route to the audition. Oh, how Cheryl will weep when she realises that her favourite contestant of that day might so very nearly not have made it because his Megabus broke down beneath a bypass in Port Talbot.

Or you can do as series four heart-throb Daniel de Bourg did. The singer hadn't even known about the auditions when he stopped off – to soak up the previous night's misdemeanours – at the centre where they were being held. *"I was on my way back from my mate's house,"* he explained, *"and wanted to stop for a burger when I saw loads of people queuing up outside this building that's really close to where I live.*

"I wondered what they were there for and then saw them all doing the 'X' sign and clicked.

"I decided to give it a shot because I had nothing better to do that day. I hadn't filled in any of the forms but luckily the producers were kind and they'd let in a few other people who hadn't got their forms with them, and let me through."

And Daniel reckons his nonchalant attitude helped to breeze him through to the finals.

"I think the best thing to do is to be down to earth and not let the audition or any of it get to you or make you feel like you're superior as that will never impress the judges.

"Just be down to earth with them and to the rest of the team. Don't go in with attitude. I didn't have a great plan in mind, I just thought I'd give it a shot."

Too right. Buddy up with crew members and be the girl/boy next door when you audition. Keep any attitude at the door. Hello success.

★ Don't rap unless you're really, really, really good at it. Rappers never fare well with the judges – perhaps because the only people who do rap on the show rap along to Noughties chart pesterers Blue or rippled pop star Peter Andre. If you need any further evidence, put "Ant and Seb Martins, Ant and Deaf, *The X Factor*" into Google and you'll soon know why.

But if you can't bear to see that again, here's a refresher. The two bros went in, all deadpan, claiming to set the world alight with their rap act.

They said: **"The X Factor *has never had anyone on it like us before. We want to become the first Welsh people to win it. [We're] confident that we can win it.*

"We've got our own style, but we're a bit like P Diddy and Usher.

*"We want to be worldwide-selling artists – we know that we are good enough."***

The brothers' mum, Clare, said: ***"Seb knows he's tone deaf but he can rap."***

Unfortunately they weren't like P Diddy or Usher and the "bit like" them extended only to the gender of the two rappers. Sadly for the boys, their rapping along to Peter Andre's sleazy 1995 hit 'Mysterious Girl' elicited tears of laughter from the judges and viewers alike and meant their dreams were blown out of the water.

There's a lesson to be learned here: get a second opinion about your talents from someone who isn't closely related, or a pal of someone closely related. It might save a lot of tears or cringing in the future.

★ Choose two songs for your audition. Otherwise, if they hate your first song, at least you can whip out an old favourite to dazzle them with.

Series two favourite Maria Lawson said: *"Go in with two song choices. I had only prepared one and they asked for another and luckily I quickly sang a Mariah Carey song I knew, but it's always good to be prepared and go in there with two songs."*

And while you're there, you might as well skip the slow-burning intro to that song.

"Also, sing the best parts of that song," says Maria. *"Just go in straight to the best bit so that you show off your voice's potential. Otherwise, they'll get bored of waiting for you to wow them.*

"Remember to look the judges in the eyes when you sing it and show them you want it more than anything. They can tell if you don't want to be there. So sing a song you're comfortable with and just enjoy it."

★ Swallow your pride and agree with Simon if necessary. Granted, if he says something unbelievably rude then stick up for yourself, but don't get flustered and say he's completely and utterly wrong about it and boy he'll be sorry, even if he is and will be. If you get through without his

approval then thank the judges and say you'll
work on your performance for next time. Otherwise,
you'll end up being one of those huffing and puffing
people who stomp their feet on the ground and
screech, "You'll be sorry Simon" through gritted
teeth and you'll receive one of Simon's despairing
sighs and be labelled as having an "attitude".
Do you really want to be that person? Do you really
want that clip on YouTube? Do you really want that
clip being brought out at every birthday from here
to eternity? Exactly.

★ Don't be too confrontational. Dreadlocked 2008
auditionee and holistic vocal coach Ariel Burdett
scared the panel half to death with her introduction.
She stomped in and tore up her number at the
judges, declaring, "I'm a human being, not a
number." When they said they didn't enjoy her song,
she called it an "academic construction" that they
weren't meant to enjoy anyway. She tried to scrap
with Cheryl and finished her unusual performance
with an earth-shattering roar. Although these
auditions tickle us, if you really want to get on in
the competition, this level of bolshiness really isn't
going to do you any favours.

★ Don't say things that you can't live up to. 2008
hopeful Ashiq Paca won the bemused looks of
Louis Walsh by saying, "I hope you feel the same
connection with my music as I do" and that his
music would heal the world. They didn't and it won't.

★ Leave the harmonica and tambourines at home.
Most people who play them during auditions look

like divs and tend to shut their eyes even more
than those without instruments. Not a good look.
But the other more important reason is that if
you zip through to Boot Camp and the live rounds,
you want to be able to whip out one of these handy
little instruments on the Singing Songs By A Worthy
Band week such as All Those Songs Coldplay Have
Written About The World Being A Bit Rubbish
Nowadays Week, Snow Patrol Do All Those Gigs
For Charity – Aren't They Nice Boys Week and U2 –
They're A Bit Right On Aren't They? Week. It will
make you look as though you have loads of little
party tricks up your sleeve – and who doesn't like a
party trick? So the lesson is, don't blow all your *X
Factor* beans at once. You'll regret it if you do.

That said, an acoustic guitar generally goes down well
with the critical crew if you can play it moderately well.
You don't need to be Eric Clapton. James Blunt will do.
Three chords are your friend and don't worry if you can't
play them too well either. You have nerves, remember –
but more of that later. The judges lapped up
Middlesbrough brothers Journey South when they came
in, all double-denim suits and co-ordinated tapping.
It's no wonder they strapped on a battered old geetar
in the third week of the live rounds.

★ NB: The acoustic guitar has another very important
purpose – it makes the string strummers look oh-so
'umble guv'nor. You can imagine them singing their
hearts out at Euston station with nothing but a flat
cap with 23p in it and a cold pasty to keep them

company. Do we think the world took notice of their heartfelt playing on their way to work? Pah, no siree. Then, all of a sudden, we feel sorry for them. They are just honest-to-God artists struggling to make ends meet in this cruel, cruel, world. Plus, they know about Real Music. The type of Real Music we like and know about – and this time round we want a "real" musician to win the show anyway.

★ TIP: Remember to mention that you're taking guitar lessons in your spare time.

HAVE A POINT TO PROVE

Piano Tie Tony, so named for daring to be the only man this side of Michael Fish to wear a tie with bold, piano-key-patterned defiance. So stark in its madness that his name – Anthony Little – was forsaken for the anguished Piano Tie Tony. Besides the aforementioned piano tie, Tony was slightly portly back then, and a wee bit bolshy. Was Simon right to label his audition "average"? Why, the hell he was, thought Tony as he stormed off. But, sadly for the Darlington chap, even shedding four stone in weight, stripping off his hateful piano tie and "working" on his personality didn't get him through. Customer services worker Tony even admitted Simon was right not to have supported him and that *still* didn't win Captain Cowell over. But at least he had A Point To Prove. People like A Point To Prove.

But not all of those with A Point To Prove have been thus disappointed. 2008 winner Alexandra came back in with A Point To Prove in series five. She'd been snubbed by

Louis first time round in 2005 and wasn't going to let that happen again.

Alexandra told MTV: *"I didn't think for a second I'd win.*

"Even when I auditioned earlier on this year, all I said to my brothers is, I want to get a step further than I did the last time... Once you're in the final 12, you deserve a tap on the back because, out of 182,000 people that applied, you've made it.

"That's all I wanted. But as the weeks went on, I got more and more hungry. I got more like, 'Oh gosh, I really really want this. I know I'm not going to win but I still want this and I'm so happy that I got given a second chance,' you know. I'm really grateful for this opportunity."

Give yourself an edge; give yourself A Point To Prove.

NERVES

Even if you're brimming with confidence, you need to show nerves at your audition. Otherwise you'll look too smug. Remember: if you're jittery you can blame any off-key notes on said jitters. You do really know "what it takes to win this competition" but are just dazzled into semi-submission by the array of illustrious judges before you.

If you don't seem nervy and waltz in there all "I'm going to be the next Leona Lewis" this and "I'm the best thing you've ever heard, Simon" that, what will you have to rely on if your singing's off? Nothing. You'll have shown them your best effort.

Poor Essex cutie Austin Drage's nerves threatened to ruin his performance in his first audition. The wee soul singer was quivering as he entered the room and burst into uncontrollable sobs when he gained the seal of approval from the judges. Try being "butterflies in the tummy" nervous rather than "can't eat, can't sleep, am going to cry in Simon Cowell's face" nervous.

THROAT INFECTIONS

A vicious throat infection assailed Laura White in the 2008 series. It helped that she had a fantastic voice – but what if she'd had an average voice? What if you have an averagely good voice? Well, infections are your friend. Remember to cough a little for authenticity and say something along the lines of, "I'm sooo gutted I had this rotten infection as I've wanted this since I was a wee nipper. Actually, better not come too close, in case I infect you too." Sorted.

Or, as a hoarse Laura croaked: *"I've been practising this audition every day for about two months and then on Saturday I woke up with this throat infection. I'm just hoping I can get through this audition."*

PRACTISE IN THE BATHROOM

No one auditioning for The X Factor uses the loo for a constitutional. They only use it for one thing – to practise. If you sing your scales in front of all the other blighters in the holding pen, then someone else might nick your song and talk over your perfectly-pitched la-la-las.

Go to the bathroom, however, and you look all serious. Your scales cannot be interrupted by the tone-deaf mumblings of those minions out back. You need peace and quiet. And mirrors of course.

Also, if you're in the bathroom, no one else can sully your footage. Go outside and you might have some other wannabe cartwheeling in the background as you tell host Dermot O'Leary about your dreams of breaking out of the nine-to-five.

BRING IN THE WORLD AND ITS MOTHER

There are basically two rules with bringing people to *The X Factor* with you. Either bring up to three people and preferably ensure one of those is a cute wee child – like Daniel Evans from 2008 – and look like you're serious and also modest, which we all know is the most important thing for *X Factor* contestants. Or bring in the world and its mother, like bubbly Welsh club singers Adante from 2008, who eventually got the axe at Boot Camp. They brought 53 supporters from North Cornelly in Wales with them. A coach load. Adante said at the time: ***"There is tumbleweed going through the village. There is no one in North Cornelly! They're all here!"***

Either be memorable for bringing an obscene number of close and personals with you or stick to a few. But just make sure that the ones you choose scream and jump up and down when you get through.

DRESS NICELY

Ceril Campbell, who is a celebrity stylist, author and

mastermind behind the Discover The New You fashion workshops, says that the talent among *X Factor* contestants should stick to nice, subtle clobber and rely on their voices to grab the attention of the judges, not their wacky togs. Piano Tie Tony, how we wish you'd known this before you auditioned.

Ceril says: *"The main thing to work out is whether you want to attract the attention of the judges for your outfit or just simply look good.*

"If you want to attract attention by your outfit, you're probably not as talented because you're relying on your flamboyant clothes and I wouldn't want to encourage anyone to dress badly for that reason.

"But if, however, you want to look good and feel confident about yourself, then follow these rules. Dress in a subtle way and make sure that you are supported in areas that need to be supported. You don't want any spillages!

"Make sure you feel confident. This means wearing shoes that you can walk in and not incredibly high heels, and wearing clothes that you like and flatter your shape.

"Look like yourself but a subtler version."

Long-locked series three runner-up Ben Mills reckons subtle styling is the way forward too.

Ben said: *"Don't style yourself.*

"Go in in plain jeans and a T-shirt and probably no make-up. You want them to think, 'We've got this average person coming in and we want to make them look like a prince or princess.'

"It makes good TV if they can see your transformation into a star and it lets the judges have an input into you. If you go in looking like a star then they have no way of developing and transforming you. I saw so many people who were styled so much and who walked out and didn't get through and I thought, 'There's no way they'll want me to go through' but they did."

But just make sure that the T-shirt is in a colour that flatters your peepers so that the focus is on your face and not on any areas from where you want to detract attention. Note of caution: remember that wearing a very light shade on top might draw attention to your chest.

Penny Sloane and Debbie Gray from Penny Sloane Associates say: *"Our eyes naturally will be drawn to the lightest area so if you're wearing all black and white shoes, the judges will look at your shoes. If you don't want attention drawn to your cleavage then be mindful that on pale skin, this can be the lightest area if you're wearing a low-cut top.*

"Wear warmer, lighter, brighter colours up near the face. A classic way of looking good is to wear a top the same shade as your eyes, which will in turn draw attention to your face.

"This is a good thing because you want the judges and voters to look where you're communicating and if you're singing, that will be your face. You want your face to be the focal point so that you look lively and engaged."

TIPS TO GET THROUGH BOOT CAMP

If you've been boosted through the auditions to Boot Camp, the key points to remember are:

★ Show another side of yourself from the one you did at auditions. If you cried at auditions, exude joy at Boot Camp and vice versa. It's a good time to show another side to your personality. Just make sure it's a good side. Austin Drage turned his nerves upside down and bopped around the stage, bringing the crowd to their feet as he trilled along to The Zutons' 'Valerie'. He cried afterwards but it didn't matter – it showed progression.

★ Sing in another language. When Spanish siren Ruth Lorenzo sang Elton John's 'Sorry Seems To Be The Hardest Word' in her mother tongue, Simon's face lit up (perhaps illuminated by thoughts of his Spanish home – or, more likely, the ringing of cash registers in Latin markets if Ruth won). It was his suggestion of course, which brings us neatly to the next point.

★ Take the judges' advice. Even if it's something small, they can see that you take on board advice and are adaptable. Oh, and be sure to tell them how useful their advice has been to you and how it has made all the difference.

★ Look a bit of a scruff so that you can have a miraculous pop star makeover and show that, wow, without the glasses and the ponytail, you're, like, really attractive. Who'd have known? Or do it t'other way around. If, like series five girl group Bad Lashes, you looked a little bit too polished in your initial audition – or as Louis put it, "like four hairdressers trying to sing" – look a bit scruffier during Boot Camp.

★ Remember to look like you're enjoying the "experience" and don't get too sucked in with trying to crawl up to the judges. Have a few good answers stored up in case the judges question your commitment, nothing too cheeky but something that shows that you are ready for "this journey". Or, as Corene from Voices With Soul puts it: "When we first entered, we just wanted to have a laugh. We said, 'We'll have an answer for Simon but we'll go along, sing as best we can and enjoy ourselves.' We thought we were going out at every stage – auditions, Boot Camp. They left us hanging to the last moment. But we just stayed ourselves, stayed bubbly and cheerful, didn't suck up and performed a song we loved and knew we sounded good on."

BOOT CAMP – THE JUDGES' HOUSES

If you've got this far, you deserve a big pat on the back. Remember, even if you don't get through, you've got a nice holiday out of it.

But back to those with a shot. Remember these points:

★ Elaborate on an earlier secret you told the judges. Music is your passion? How nice? Stuff that for a game of soldiers. Singing is your passion because it's the only thing that got you through your beloved pet hamster Gerald dying, and make sure your assigned judge knows it.

★ Size up the competition and be sure to offer your support – genuine or not – to the other contestants. You want to give as much time as possible for your relationship with them to develop into "best friends" and also you want those rejected to tip you as the one to watch in interviews.

★ Jump in the pool like series two contestant Chico Slimani did when he was told he was going through to the final 12. This shows how much fun you are to be around and gives the producers a good clip to use in your montage. But make sure you don't take the live microphone in with you like the ex-goatherd did despite being a trained electrician. Chico told *Metro: "I wanted to be famous but I didn't plan to get 5,000 volts of electricity through me and become famous for being that dead guy in Sharon Osbourne's swimming pool.*

"We all had to sing around Sharon's pool and I saw people like Ozzy and Rachel Hunter watching, going crazy, and I just got carried away. Little did I know I could have fried myself. I look back and think I deserved to do well in The X Factor *because I went through a lot. I could have electrocuted myself."*

★ Always ring up your family on your phone and scream down it regardless of the cost of international calls. Them's the rules.

★ Always cry for those who didn't get through, to show how sensitive you are.

★ Thank your judge for "this opportunity" and say how much this means to you. You might as well throw in an "I can't believe this is happening to me" every now and again as well to show how down to earth you still are. There's nice.

HOW TO WIN X FACTOR

chapter three

SONG CHOICE

*"If you can have a story behind a ballad –
you know, this is the one my mum used to
sing me when I was a child – then you have
a recipe for success."*

In the land of *The X Factor*, song choice is king. If you hit
a bum note but sing a well-loved classic you could be
spared the axe, but sing a turkey perfectly and you could
be on your way home.

As chuffing obvious as it sounds, you want to make sure
that what you're singing suits your voice and your style
but also shows that you're not afraid to experiment. In her
second week, Diana Vickers stepped away from the
Damien Rice and Dido covers to sing 'Man In The Mirror'
in Michael Jackson week, which was regarded as her
best performance during her stay and, crucially, made
her look adaptable. Later on in the contest, Diana was
criticised for being too samey week after week.

Better times ... Series one winner Steve Brookstein headlines the show's tour in 2005.
(SONY MUSIC ARCHIVE/GETTY IMAGES)

Number what? ... Series one runners-up G4 celebrate going to number one in the album charts by sticking their fingers up. (JO HALE/GETTY IMAGES)

Cowell and co ... Louis Walsh, ex-judge Sharon Osbourne and Simon Cowell in 2006. (SHOWBIZIRELAND/GETTY IMAGES)

Snapped ... Series two runner-up Andy Abraham at a premiere in 2005.
(GARETH CATTERMOLE/GETTY IMAGES)

Sweet and greet ... Second series character Chico Slimani chats to fan Matthew Johnson,
who is allergic to virtually every food type, at the *Woman's Own* 'Children of Courage
Awards' in 2005. (TIM GRAHAM/GETTY IMAGES)

Drip ... Chico Slimani shows that his days as a male stripper weren't for nothing.
(ANDY STUBBS/WIREIMAGE)

Ok With Us ... Series two winner Shayne Ward shows off his pop star pout in a publicity picture taken in 2007. (DAN TUFFS/GETTY IMAGES)

Not hair for much longer ... Series three finalist Ben Mills has his much-loved locks cut by Nicky Clarke weeks after the final. (GETTY IMAGES)

Quinning look ... Series three runner-up Ray Quinn melts hearts by posing with his grandmother Marjorie before doing some instore signings in his native Liverpool in 2007. (DAVE HOGAN/GETTY IMAGES)

A Moment Like This ... Series three winner and international star Leona Lewis laps up the hometown glory at the Hackney Empire in 2006. (KEN MCKAY/REX FEATURES)

Oh how the times have changed ... Ray Quinn enjoys his instore signing for his eponymous debut album at the now defunct Woolworths in 2007. Who would have thought Ray Quinn would outlive Woolies? (DAVE HOGAN/GETTY IMAGES)

Bleeding heck ... Leona Lewis on set in New York for her 2007 single 'Bleeding Love' which went on to top the charts in 34 countries. (THEO WARGO/GETTY IMAGES)

"Every week you come out and do the same thing, Diana," moaned Louis at the time. *"You never do any dancing or anything. To have* The X Factor *you need to have it all. The other girls are more versatile."*

And Diana herself admitted to ITV that she was biting her nails about singing a song that probably wasn't written with a 17-year-old girl in mind.

Diana quivered: *"I was so scared of performing 'Man In The Mirror' and it turned out to be one of my best."*

So bear in mind when choosing songs that a well-placed musical U-turn can pique interest in you for weeks to come. Even series four hunk Daniel de Bourg conceded that although he didn't like the choice of 'Build Me Up Buttercup' by The Foundations for his final week, it is good to show a bit of range in your abilities and show you can master those songs that are out of your usual remit.

Daniel said: *"Song choice is everything so stick to your guns with it.*

"I wanted to do more acoustic music because that's what I love but I did something more up-tempo for movies week.

"I didn't especially like the song and I did say so, but at the end of the day, you have to show that you can do other types of music and it's good to do a song that makes people smile or gets them moving.

"It didn't work that well for me in the end as I left that week but you do have to show compromise and be willing to try songs you wouldn't usually. Just make sure you voice your concerns in a constructive way in the week. Don't leave it until the live show to moan about it or you'll look foolish. And respect what the judges have to say on the night because between them they have a lot of knowledge and experience.

"If you feel it isn't working when you're on stage, just make the best of it and enjoy being up there. You might as well and then at least you've entertained people. You don't want to look back on the whole experience and remember how much you didn't enjoy it, because otherwise you shouldn't be doing it."

Once you've set aside time for a constructive chat with your mentor and voice coach about song possibilities, be sure to remember to throw in a few modern hits to the table – or at least ways of making a golden oldie bang up to date.

Ben Mills confirmed: *"Song choice is so important. You've got to have the right songs. You could win* The X Factor *on song choice alone, and really the judges could decide who they want to win the show just on the right choices.*

"If you're going to sing one of Mariah Carey's biggest hits on the live show, then you'll probably go through to the next round. If you're going to do older songs then people might respect you more, but those people might not vote for you because they might not be the type of people who vote for TV shows."

Series one group Voices With Soul also reckon that you're just as well singing a popular and modern song so that you can prove you're capable of doing songs that reach the Top 10.

Grace from Voices With Soul said: *"You should choose a modern song that you can put your own spin on like Hope did with 'Umbrella' by Rihanna in 2007.*

"That way, the song is in the public's consciousness anyway and should be in the charts or has recently been in the charts and consequently is already well-liked with the people who watch the show. You want to perform songs that people care about and show them how you would treat the same song.

"You want them to be able to sing along and get your version in their heads.

"However, if you pick a fuddy-duddy song that people don't care about or haven't heard for ages, then they won't be able to picture what types of songs you'll be putting out in the future, and that makes you harder to market and harder for people to be able to warm to and understand what you're about as an act."

So once you've found a song that is slightly out of your "comfort zone", modern and popular, you might as well start thinking of the meaning behind it. Go on, have a good think about what that song means to you. Does it remind you of the time you caught the love of your life having it off with your Uncle Billy in the back of a yellow

Ford Cortina? Does that make you feel like crying? Well, you'd better relieve yourself of the burden of carrying that hurt by yourself and let us at home know all about it before you sing it. A problem shared is a problem halved – and your votes quadrupled.

Ben Mills said: *"If you can have a story behind a ballad – you know, this is the one my mum used to sing me when I was a child – then you have a recipe for success.*

"People like to be able to understand the motivations behind your song choices as it gives them another incentive to take interest in you and hopefully vote for you."

And if you have no raw emotion behind a song, you might as well pretend you do and choose a song that will cause people watching to cry into their receivers as they dial away your number to keep you in the contest.

Ben Mills continued: *"There's two types of emotions for songs – the emotions that make you happy like 'All You Need Is Love' by The Beatles or the ones that make you sad like 'I Don't Want To Miss A Thing' by Aerosmith.*

"If you can make people feel happy or sad then you're on to a winner. You want to do songs that people associate with those feelings and the ones that have a special place in their hearts, for example the types of songs people play at weddings or at funerals."

"But if you don't make them feel either of those things, then you'll be at a loose end because the chances are that most

people won't attach a special significance to the song and won't be able to connect with it as instantly.

"Sharon gave me U2's 'Still Haven't Found What I'm Looking For' in the, finals which is a great song but it doesn't wrench any of those emotions. So when I walked out singing it, the nation probably thought – what the hell?

"He still *doesn't know what he's looking for? He's been in this show for weeks now and he still has no clue, why should we vote for him? And you can't blame them for thinking that because the song doesn't appeal to either of those emotions."*

So stick with emotional songs that have some meaning to you – or have a universal meaning easily understood by the great British public. Use songs that you sound good on and stretch yourself if it sounds right but don't be different for the sake of it – it'll look strained otherwise and people will have trouble understanding what musical path you want to follow. Or you'll sound rubbish.

If you hate your song choice on the night, then try and keep it to yourself and make the best of it like Daniel de Bourg did. Keep your body language positive so at least you look as if you're having a jolly good craic instead of looking as if you've just squirted your eyeballs with vinegar.

Author of *Body Language For Dummies* and director of Kuhnke Communications, Elizabeth Kuhnke, says: *"The contestants who do well in* **The X Factor** *are those who* *know how to be authentic to themselves and who are comfortable with that.*

"Keep your gestures simple when the cameras are on you. It can be distracting for viewers if you're all over the place. Likewise don't be too flamboyant when you're performing as that's off-putting. Move with purpose so when you do make a gesture, there's meaning behind it.

"While you're singing in the live shows, claim your space on the stage. You've got the right to be on that stage. The stages are terrifying and really huge but remember that you've earned the right to be there and demonstrate that."

Series two contestant Maria Lawson is all too aware of how important it is to be confident on stage. *"When you're on the stage, you just have to enjoy it and forget about the cameras,"* she confirms.

"It is a huge deal because there are so many people watching, but don't let it get to you. Keep smiling and enjoy it."

So now you have your body language sorted and know which types of songs to go for, keep in mind these things:

★ Hold out for songs that have *X Factor* buzzwords in them. These are: "love", "loss", "dream", "moment", "chance", "second chance", "mountain", "barriers", "against all odds", "always" and "eternal". If in doubt, go to Hallmark and take a note of the words used in birthday cards for grandparents. Job's a good 'un.

It might also be worth considering hiring a children's choir of especially cherub-faced children to totter on stage with you. Who wants to be the old miser who wasn't moved by the lisping, pre-pubescent voices of some little tykes? Same Difference made sure their Christmas song in the final was as delightful as possible and tugged at the heartstrings of us voters by bringing on some rosy-cheeked nippers dressed as elves. The cheery pair also visited a school in the week leading up to the final for a quick sing-song with the excited kiddies and brought out another children's choir for their cuddly version of 'I Have A Dream' with Jason Donovan, just like Abba did all those years ago, and it certainly worked for them. All together now: ahh!

Not to be outdone in the final, Rhydian sang 'O Holy Night' with a gospel choir *and* a children's choir in a sugary appearance that put sweet-voiced eventual winner Leon Jackson in the shade.

But remember to refuse the children's choir if things are already looking too corny. Series five group Girlband were left looking schmaltzy when they performed Michael Jackson's 'Heal The World' in angelic white dresses, a choir of young women and a montage of the world in the background. Simon snubbed the song, saying it was ***"gimmicky"*** and ***"only missing polar bears and a chorus of children".*** Later, they said they regretted the cheesy production, and had been asked to come out with animals and a children's choir but thought that would be taking the idea too far.

Phoebe Lau from Girlband said: *"They actually wanted to give us a whole children's choir with them holding gerbils and hamsters and we said no.*

"Imagine if the rabbits had actually been on stage!"

So if you feel uncomfortable with the production and you feel it's too cheesy, then say before it's too late. Likewise, make sure your togs suit the song you're singing. If you're going to be performing an energetic number with lots of bopping around the stage, you don't want your chest spilling out.

Celebrity stylist, author and brains behind the Discover The New You workshops, Ceril Campbell, says: *"You want to grab the judges' and public's attention for the right reasons."*

Bear in mind that the camera might make you look heftier than you are and while there's nothing wrong with more flesh, if you feel uncomfortable about it and are constantly fidgeting with your arms, bear in mind that you might look anxious and people, in turn, might interpret that as you being a right old grumpy so and so.

Ceril says: *"It's true that the camera adds at least 7lbs so don't wear anything that's going to draw attention to areas you don't like. Stay clear of really short skirts unless you have fantastic legs and want attention drawn to them.*

"Another tip for X Factor contestants is to make sure you look at yourself from all angles in the mirror with your

stage outfit because you never know where the camera is going to focus on."

Indeed. So get your Whitney and Mariah hits nailed, practise, practise, practise in front of the mirror with your stage clothes on and then watch those votes come flooding in for you once you perform. You made it on your own. Well done.

chapter four

HOMETOWN GLORY

"When we switched on the Christmas lights in Luton, we had the biggest crowd ever – the council told us."

Hail from a bog-standard town or city where everyone knows your name? Born in an area so mediocre that the only way to wriggle through the tedium of youth in your pleasant but dull excuse for home was by singing in local talent shows?

Good on you my friend; you've just got yourself entry to the next level of *The X Factor's* winner's circle.

At face value, being cheered on by a bunch back home – who remember you only as the precocious child who wiped your nose on your sleeve and warbled 'Amazing Grace' at any and every school concert going – probably seems like a poor idea. But wait. Get the backing of a town or, even better, a region and you're laughing.

Spiky-haired Derry teen Eoghan Quigg, who came third in 2008, had all of Northern Ireland rooting for him. Ruth Lorenzo from the same series had all of Spain. And what of leather-jacket fiends JLS? Well, they had all of Croydon raining hosannas upon them.

Grace Campbell, from series one finalists Voices With Soul, remembered: *"We had all of Luton and Bedfordshire, as well as Buckinghamshire and Hampshire. All the shires really! It made things so much easier, having the support of people back home while we were on and off the show. When we switched on the Christmas lights in Luton, we had the biggest crowd ever – the council told us."*

Ruth Lorenzo told Digital Spy: *"I appreciate every single vote I've had. I've had votes from grandmas, from 14-year-olds spending their pocket money, housewives, men, just about everyone."*

Carl Pemberton, from series two band of brothers Journey South, said: *"The support we had in our home town was truly amazing.*

"We didn't realise the extent of our popularity until we came home during the semi-final of The X Factor and witnessed the streets of Middlesbrough town centre lined with thousands upon thousands of people all there for us.

"The support we received gave us even more of a reason to do well to make our town proud and put it on the map."

So what is it about local support that is so important for *The X Factor?* Well, it works in a number of ways...

★ If they like you there's less chance of cringe-worthy stories being leaked to the press. Only a real scum bucket would shop in the girl who spent every Saturday of her youth packing grannies' bags down at Morrisons for having bad BO as a teen. Therefore, make friends with everyone in town and make everyone want to be nice about you. If you get picked to go through to the final 12 then you can bet your bottom dollar that your local news programme will film local people on the busiest street in your town and ask them what type of person you are. So give them plenty to work with. A bit of charity collecting or patting whey-faced children lightly on the head will probably stand you in good stead.

★ Once you're in the final 12, you'll need "the people back home" to pick up their phones and vote for you every week. They'll want a stake in your success. Let them have it, that's fine. Mention how amazing those very same people have been to you throughout your singing career. How they've always supported you. How it was so hard growing up in that town as it had so very few places where you could perform but that they always gave you a chance. And that chance, that generous chance, meant you were able to give *The X Factor* a whirl. Thank them, go on, do it – "sincerely" – from the bottom of your heart. Say that the next song is for them. Bingo.

Series three star Ben Mills said: ***"I had an amazing amount of support, especially in Kent where I'm from.***

"People couldn't believe a guy from Kent was on The X Factor *and they were really supportive of me. They felt I was doing it for them as well as for me. I used to do a lot of chats with people on Kent radio shows just to keep up a good relationship with people at home and still people at home are really kind and encouraging of me."*

★ NB: If it all goes belly up, you'll need them to turn up when you switch on the town's Christmas lights two years after you first appeared in the show, so make nice.

Leona Lewis found time after her 2006 victory to pay tribute to her East London roots. *"I am really proud to be a Hackney girl,"* she told the, erm, *Hackney Gazette*, *"and appreciate all the support you have given me."* She even played a hometown gig at the Hackney Empire.

Two years later, now a globe-straddling superduperstar, she remained an EastEnder at heart: *"It's quite a down to earth place; it keeps me really grounded. They're all normal people like myself and I went to school in that area... All my family lives there. So it's nice when you come back – I can see them and spend time with them."*

Indeed, it's a rare weekend that you don't see LL swigging a can of Fanta at a Hackney bus stop, or practising bunny hops on her bicycle outside the Town Hall."

So you need to show a little face. Be seen on your to-camera piece going home and cutting the ribbon of the new post office or, better still, old folks' home. Get a few nice old biddies in the shot with you and show how polite you are – not like those hooligan hoodie yoofs in the news. Diana Vickers and her family played a blinder by keeping in regular touch with their Blackburn buddies and the local press, thus making sure the pretty teen was a constant fixture in the local media.

Most professional public relations experts would have been impressed when councillor Michael Law-Riding became especially keen on putting on a small concert with Diana as the star when she returned home. This did no end of good in sustaining the feeling of goodwill for the northern lass.

Michael said at the time: ***"Obviously we were disappointed that Diana did not get through to* The X Factor final.**

"However we are exploring what options are open to us so that we can make sure Diana gets the recognition she deserves from her friends and loyal fans in her home town."

Reminiscences of the rose-tinted variety are always good for bonus points. If your family moved to a bigger house during your childhood you should consider going back to the old, smaller house, especially if it's on the wrong side of the tracks, though even if it is perfectly nice it'll do. You want to show your "humble" roots. Reflect on this by temporarily taking hint from *EastEnders* actors when given a scene of "quiet reflection". Revisit the local park on a day when there's a slight drizzle. Be filmed sitting on a swing looking moodily into the distance, a light breeze fanning that loose lock of hair that's escaped from your Alice band, and dark satanic mills in the background, while a tot the same sex as you and with roughly the same shade hair is playing nicely nearby.

Give a "shout out" to a football team back home. Know a semi-professional Conference team that is about to have the stuffing knocked out of them at a local derby? Well mention that your song is for them and put on "your" side's badge. A scarf might be taking it a bit too far and also might be in unflattering colours.

Multiply your chances of success by mentioning any other areas where you've lived, worked or studied in – or where your family has, if you haven't. The always well-prepared Rhydian Roberts set a fine example in this regard. He studied at the Conservatoire in Birmingham but made telling references to his home in Wales. It might have been our chocolate-fuelled imagination but we swear he even talked in Welsh at one point. If you can speak another language, especially Welsh, try asking people to vote for you in that language. If nothing else, it will make you sound exotic and intelligent.

Talk in a broader accent when you're "back home" to show that you haven't lost your roots. The queen of this specialist celebrity skill is Lulu – Scots popstress and Take That's mum – who breaks into a broad East Dunbartonshire lilt whenever she's on a chat show and speaks about her family. Prove that, inside, you're still the same, very humble, wannabe pop star.

Invite lots of people from your hometown to appear in the audience. Get a few teachers, a few nice old ladies, some cool-looking young guns and some cute children.
These can represent a cross-section of your community, and send the message that all the town's teachers, nice old ladies, young guns and children like you. Get them to wear printed T-shirts with a winning picture of you accompanied with an obvious pun on your name.
If you're rather charming, you might want to try asking them to each wear a different initial on the back of their tee so that during your song, the camera can pan around to their backs emblazoned with your name.

Soulful second series contestant Maria Lawson said:
"It was really helpful having my family and friends in the audience every week. They made banners and T-shirts, and just having them there made me feel great and pushed me on to do better." Even now, the first paragraph of Maria's official biography pays tribute to her "down to earth" nature.

Another tried-and-tested tactic is to ensure that a significant loved one misses quite a few of your performances, so that you can make a big deal of them popping up on the show. Quite understandably, Ruth Lorenzo's Spanish family couldn't be there every week at the live shows. So, when they *did* crop up, all the judges banged on about how she'd sung her heart out for her beloved kin. *"It means so much to know my family are here tonight,"* Ruth said on the show, melting hearts across the nation.

Mention places where you used to sing and perform in your local community and then drop them into conversation. This is a particularly effective ruse when the opportunity arises in conversations with Big and Famous People. Cue: "Hello Mrs J. Lo. Wow, this studio is so amazing. It's three times as big as my parents' semi-detached, three-bedroomed house in Lichfield." This gives the oh-so Big and Famous Person a chance to show how dead common they are too and how they came from a house that only had one television – can you believe it? We, in return, will warm to them even more and immediately purchase their latest CD. Everyone's a winner!

This brings us not so neatly to another ready-made route to victory: mentioning a local – or near enough – famous person done good. They've probably got a book or an album or a TV series out and could do with your support as much as you could with theirs. If any popular, former *X Factor* contestants are from the same area as you, shout it out. Having their approval will help cement your worthiness in the competition. If they are doing any local concerts, get your name on the bill. You being fresh-faced and from the telly will help.

Gary Barlow went positively cuckoo over fellow flaxen northerner Diana Vickers when he did a masterclass with the teen on the show. ***"If Simon doesn't sign you,"*** honked the Take Thatter, ***"I will!"*** And if you have Gary Barlow's seal of approval, it's fair to assume that most *X Factor* voters will be ripe for the picking.

Make friends with the local media. Be nice to journalists, radio and TV crews. They'll be the ones who'll keep your profile up if you don't win the show. You might also want to consider setting up your own website or MySpace page so that fans can get in touch and you can spill favourable news about yourself across the internet.

"I'm still on good terms with local radio stations and media," points out Ben Mills. *"They'll get me to do a live session for them or comment on* The X Factor. *I think it's a good idea to have good relations with local media. They can help you out and you can help them out."*

If you've done all this, give yourself a gold star.

HOW TO WIN X FACTOR

chapter five

NEVER EVER BE IN A BAND

"Bands are less focused on individual characters, and it is difficult to know who to care about."

Bands never seem to get on well in *The X Factor*. And there's a jolly good reason for that. Same Difference – a Nineties teen put-down. JLS – an insurance company. Girlband – *Girl Band*. 2 To Go – open goal. It's simple really. Their names are utter tripe.

Granted, there's not much in the way of rich pickings in the great band names department in the charts anyway. Arctic Monkeys? The Pigeon Detectives? Oasis? Nonetheless, you get the feeling that those acts have put a wee bit more effort – however misguided – into their monikers than the majority of those on *The X Factor*.

Maybe this is because many of the bands on *The X Factor* haven't been together for long, but this is

no excuse for a ho-hum name or for us to pity them.
They're going on TV, for goodness' sakes. *TV*. And some
of them flounce up with a name that is akin to a "kick
me" sign.

Really, is it any wonder no band has won *The X Factor*
with names like this?
2 To Go
4Tune
Addictiv Ladies
4Sure
Eton Road
*(although at least these fellas had the foresight to use
a name that could easily be used on promotional street
signs with any future releases)*
Hope
Same Difference
JLS
Girlband

And what of the better names in the show? Well, they
haven't really been that great either.
Journey South
Voices With Soul
Futureproof
Bad Lashes

Come on people! If you're going to audition as a band
and want to give yourselves the best possible shot on
the show, Justin Rubaloff, owner and developer of
BandNameMaker.com, has the answer. He reckons
the best bet is to have a good think about the type of

music you'll be singing and what message you want to give to people:

"I feel the best way to come up with a name is to let your band's music and style evolve. Finding a name should be the least of your worries as a band on The X Factor.

"Remember that the goal of your band should be to have fun, write good music, and sing well together.

"And if the name you've chosen doesn't suit, you can play live with a temporary name. I've known some bands that changed their name on every gig because they couldn't settle.

"You don't have to name your band directly after the type of music you play, but the name shouldn't work against your style either. Go to billboard.com and look at the new releases list – pay attention to the names you don't know and try to imagine what style of music it is."

By the same token, you don't want to simply go for the bleedin' obvious. Yes, we're looking at you, "Girlband". At least Voices With Soul seemed to have spent more than five minutes conjuring up a name, even if they did end up sounding like they'd looted leftovers from Nineties girl group SWV (Sisters With Voices).

Justin continues: *"Try brainstorming – have each band member write down five words that describe the feeling, mood, or style of your music. You might find that two of these words joined together make a perfect name.*

Or, at the very least, the list of words gets you thinking of new ideas.

"Narrow your list of names and ask friends and family that have heard your band to look them over. Use online band name generators. BandNameMaker.com is particularly useful because it lets you type in a word to use in the random generation process.

"But mainly don't stress if the name you chose isn't sticking or if you change your mind. Many famous bands changed their names multiple times after they began playing live." (Just ask The Quarrymen, The Silver Beatles or, as they eventually became known, that band from Liverpool.) (No, not Atomic Kitten.)

It's a good idea to try to avoid difficult names that are hard to get ingrained into fans' heads.

"Because a name might work well for one particular band and not another makes it difficult to define a general rule," says Justin. *"However, for X Factor bands, my advice would be to avoid band names that are the same or similar as an existing band's.*

"You also want to avoid excessively long names – although there are professional bands with long names – and excessively clever names, as these can be annoying or off-putting.

"Also, avoid words that are difficult to spell. Assuming one of the goals of your band is to "get famous", you'll need to

use a basic marketing skill along with everything else that goes with being a good band. Words that are difficult to spell will make it harder for your fans to find you on the web."

So, there's the band name sorted. What about the rest?

Well it's not just the dross names that are doing the bands no favours. It's their styling on the show. Girlband, all ravishing young ladies, were made to look like four Quality Street sweets on their first week, with huge, shiny, garish dresses. JLS wore a series of increasingly bad leather jackets and were each ascribed a primary colour to wear every week. Admittedly, while sartorially reprehensible, this made it easier for fans to wear their favourite member's colour. But did those cows really die to be made into a boxy, mustard yellow leather bomber jacket? We think not. So be honest with your stylist if your look doesn't seem to be working.

Image experts Penny Sloane and Debbie Grays at Penny Sloane Associates say: *"If you get through to the final 12 and have a stylist, make sure you understand your strengths and don't go down the road they want to take you down if it doesn't feel comfortable for you.*

"Stick to your guns. You know what works for you and what works for the band. So make sure you tell the stylists that and be honest, so that they can work with you all and come up with something flattering for the band."

But is it just a matter of styling and bad names that is holding back our bands or is it something more fundamental? Or is it, perchance, Louis Walsh, who usually mentors the bands? Peter Robinson, editor of online music site Popjustice, thinks so:

"Louis Walsh is really ineffectual as a mentor.

"On TV, he comes across as a bit naff and a bit rubbish even though he's massively successful and does know about pop music.

"He's always seen as the bad mentor to be lumped with. He has trouble standing up to Cheryl Cole and she's only been there a year. Because of this, it's hard to see how he'll fight battles for his bands and, consequently, people don't warm to him at home because he doesn't seem very engaging or effective."

So if you are a band who gets left with Louis, make sure that – unless you want to be the next Westlife – you leave the white suits, schmaltzy Michael Bublé covers and stools at home.

In fairness to Louis, he was an exceptionally good promoter for JLS, landing them a topless shoot in *Heat* magazine, which was doubtless enjoyed by their fan base. He selflessly travelled up and down London in a brightly coloured JLS hoodie, sitting aboard a bus decked out with the JLS logo. Bellowing *"Vote JLS"* at the top of his lungs into a megaphone. Simon Cowell didn't do that. Neither did Dannii or Cheryl. So, if you do get Louis, and you're in a band, make sure you play to his strengths and use his experience. (The wee fella has after all presided over more chart-topping singles than… well, you and me anyway.)

Another problem with being in a band is the divided loyalties syndrome. It is definitely harder for the audience to connect with a band because there are too many of you to concentrate on, whereas a solo performer will get our undivided attention. It's harder to care about you because there's too much going on. Think, if you're in doubt, of series four band Hope. Six members to begin with and then five. (They were whittled down to five after it was revealed that member Sisi Jghalef had an unspent community service order. Crikey.) It seemed like hard work to remember their names, let alone get to know them well enough to pick up the phone and vote for them each week.

"Bands are less focused on individual characters," confirms Peter Robinson, *"and it is difficult to know who to care about and whose story to follow in the band. It's OK if there's just two or three members, but any more and there's no focus."*

You would do well to take a leaf out of Spice Girls' book and work out who'll be the one to twist their ankles wearing skyscraper heels, who'll be the mouthy one who'll try and start fights with Liam Gallagher, who'll be the one who points at the camera, who'll be the one to screech "zig-a-zig-ah" and who will be the other one. Or you can pick up the pop baton from All Saints and work out who will be the ones to fall out over a khaki jacket and thus create a controversy as well.

If you can assign roles now, you have time to perfect them before you go into the live finals and help the voting public get to know you.

Grace Campbell from Voices With Soul said: *"As a band, you have to decide each week who will be taking the lead vocals.*

"You have to do the best for your band, so choose the best singer for that song. And make sure you work on your harmonies throughout, otherwise you'll sound all over the place, which will sound terrible on live TV."

So there you have it.

chapter six

MAKING FRIENDS WITH OTHER CONTESTANTS

"We're all one big happy family."

Ahh, aren't the *X Factor* lot nice? They're always hugging each other and saying how well they all get on. Why, they're just like one big happy family. Indeed, they see each other as sisters and brothers from another mother. They've met each other's families. They love each other, which means so much. And, whatever happens in this competition, they've made loads of friends along the way and will stay pals with them long after the show has finished.

Bona fida buddies or complete balderdash for the cameras, it's a pretty good idea to be as pally with as many contestants and crew as possible to get ahead in the competition.

Diana Vickers said of her not-really-love-interest Eoghan Quigg in series five: *"Me and Eoghan are best friends.*

"We've got such a strong bond. People forget that we're similar ages – I'm only nine months older than him. I'm just a kid still, we're both still studying, and we've got the same sense of humour."

And series four was no less chummy, according to 2007 contestant Daniel de Bourg. *"I made friends with absolutely everybody,"* he said.

"The contestants, the crew, the people behind the scenes, everybody. They can tell if you're fake immediately. They've seen it all before and they play a big part in how you're presented. It also makes the whole thing much nicer if you're friends with more people on the show.

"I'm still friends with loads of those people now – and it was nearly two years ago that I was on the programme."

Just imagine what might happen if a contestant waltzed in and immediately accused the other acts of being backstabbing little gits with odour issues and bad breath in the morning? It might be funny to hear, but eventually the audience will boo and hiss – and, more likely than not, vote you off at the earliest opportunity. After all, who wants to spend their Saturday evenings watching a socially awkward crosspatch?

Consequently, very few contestants *have* whizzed in and said they dislike their comrades. 2008 hopeful Rachel Hylton proved a rare exception, making no bones about her lack of affinity with her rivals when she left the show. At her press conference, she said: *"I definitely felt isolated from the other contestants because I didn't live in the house."* (She had, quite reasonably, opted to remain with her small children.)

"When you've got a group of people and you're lonely in a crowded room, that's not a good feeling. I wasn't really close to any of the other contestants – I knew them, I'd say hi, but I wasn't close."

Rachel elaborated on this to *This Morning*: *"To be honest, none of them were really my friends. I could've used some support when I was at my lowest points in the show. They all support each other. They were all close to each other – but nobody had any time for me."*

When the contestants bang on about being great pals, perhaps it's because they do all get along and are going through the same "journey". Or perhaps it's because they've got savvy.

"We don't like ruthless people," says Phillip Hodson, who is a Fellow of the British Association for Counselling and Psychotherapy. *"We like winners but winners who win nicely.*

"As such, it's useful to become friends with other contestants on The X Factor; *not just because you're going through a similar thing, but because you want to show human emotion again.*

"If they win or get through to another round and you don't, you want to be able to show that you're a nice person and smile, even if it is just through gritted teeth."

Voices With Soul, finalists in the first series, said:
"We made friends with everyone on that show and treated everyone the same.

"We're bubbly girls and we were bubbly to everyone because if you treat people like rubbish on the way up, people remember. We didn't treat anyone as any better than anyone else – and, luckily, everyone still remembers us as the bubbly group from the first series."

So while it's a great idea to be friendly with all of the team, you might want to size all the contenders up. Be nice to all but keep your eyes peeled for your biggest rival and the strongest contestant in the show. Your best bet is to pal up with the person most likely to win the show. There are abundant good reasons for this philanthropy.

★ If they are the most popular person in the show, then your being friends with them will rub off on their fans. The voting public will duly believe that, as the popular contestant clearly has great taste, you must be a jolly good egg.

As their new best friend, you can say things on screen like how you think they're better than you and deserve to win more than you do. This demonstrates that not only are you a good chum, but you're also humble. Hopefully, they'll say the same during their bit to camera and some of their voters will trust their opinion and vote for you. Then, if they get the axe, they'll tip you as the winner and you will in turn inherit their fans.

After being given the boot Diana Vickers was seen wearing a Vote Eoghan T-shirt. This fuelled speculation about whether or not they were in a relationship, and encouraged her fans to nail their colours to the Quigg mast.

"I want Eoghan to win," Diana told ITV at the time. *"He's such an amazing boy. He puts everything into his performances."*

This made her look like a good loser and helped her chances of remaining appealing to the public after the competition ended.

You can show your wonderfully caring side through the medium of these new pals. You cry because they're given the boot and, all of a sudden, we realise how sensitive you are. *"When Ruth left, I cried,"* Alexandra told BBC Radio 1. *"It's best friends. Me and Ruth were best friends, Diana and Eoghan are best friends. And that's how it is, when you lose your best friends."*

Plus you can reveal that you're actually really hilarious and fun to be around. The finalists, tired of hearing Austin Drage's harmonica, "misplaced" the instrument to stop him playing it 24/7. Gentle rib-tickling banter with JLS promptly ensued.

With a bit of luck, these new pals will stick up for you when journalists dismiss you in interviews. After being given the surprise chop in favour of Rachel Hylton staying in the show, Austin Drage sweetly defended Daniel Evans honour at his press conference, suggesting that he had as much right to be in the show as any of the other contestants after the judges bemoaned Daniel for escaping the firing line.

Austin said: *"I don't think people called up to vote for Daniel out of sympathy. He's a lovely, lovely man and the public can see that."*

Let's face it, you're going to look like a bit of a prat if you have to spend all of your time telling the world how great you are; much better that a casual observer does that and leaves you to look like the injured party in it all.

Finally, bear in mind that if your new best *X Factor* friend gets big and famous and you don't, they might invite you to support them on tour. Or if not on tour, you might be able to jet off on swanky holidays with them, as Ruth Lorenzo did with Alexandra Burke who went to Mauritius after Christmas. Nice.

HOW TO WIN X FACTOR

chapter seven

SOB STORIES

"It made me a stronger person."

Ding, dong it's sob o' clock!

Winning *The X Factor* is as much about being able to tell a tragic tale as it is about mastering 'Candle In The Wind'. Even though many viewers have berated sob stories on fan forums, they still seem to be wheeled out at an alarming rate.

Even the judges have said that they're sick of sad stories accompanied by much sobbing, but that doesn't seem to stop our sensitive singers.

Louis Walsh was certainly peeved about it, telling *The Mirror*, **"The public has been going for these sob stories and the acts go for the sympathy vote. There were far too many sob stories and far too much crying in series four. This is supposed to be a talent show, not Jeremy Kyle. With Same Difference, it was crying,** *not the singing, that has got them in the final. This has to change."*

For once, Simon Cowell agreed with Louis (albeit not about Same Difference). As series five loomed, he told *The Sunday Mirror*: *"We are attempting to move away from focusing too much on the sob stories. This year, it's all about trying to go back to raw talent. The stories got out of hand and people were starting not to believe them. It had got to the stage that people were trying harder to gain sympathy than to get praise for their singing."*

Nevertheless, fresh waves of sob stories crashed into series five. The fact is, they work on *The X Factor* because it's an over-the-top emotional show and we want over-the-top emotion. (That's why no one's been tempted to cover Kraftwerk yet.) Those who don't reveal or show any flicker of feeling are usually punished.

Axed at Boot Camp, Welsh ex-golfer James Williams told *Wales on Sunday* that the reason he wasn't put through to the final 12 was because he didn't have any traumatic tales to tell the judges: *"I am disappointed that I got down from hundreds of thousands of people to the last 24 and then wasn't even on the TV for a minute. Someone who lived down the street said to me, 'There's a guy that looks like you on* The X Factor.*' How bad is that? We've joked about the fact that if I had said I had tried committing suicide I would have featured more."*

Series three runner-up Ben Mills said: *"My tip is what Mark Hudson, my vocal coach, used to say to me and that was to beat the crap out of fellow finalist Ray Quinn and shag Leona Lewis!*

"It's extreme, but he said you'd get people and the media going crazy over it because you don't have any particularly sad stories to tell, and he had a very good point in that you have to make sure that you work the media as much as you can.

"Especially the way it's going nowadays on the show… like if your mum is dying or your pet rat has just died, then you're best to talk about it on the show and sing a song about it with a montage of your pet rat in the background.

"It's a lot of dedicating songs to people and saying, 'If I don't win this my house will be repossessed'. But with me, I owned my own marquee company, which was doing fine, so there was no way anyone was going to feel sorry for me over that… why would they?

"You have to remember that The X Factor *is a game and it is a competition and sometimes it seems like it's a competition between who's having the worst luck at that moment and how you exploit that."*

You don't have to threaten to leap off a tall building or have a run of bad luck to get through. However, it might help your chances if you can reveal a sad but universal experience that you've encountered and that singing – your passion – got you through it. And, of course, made you the strong, well-rounded contestant that you are today.

There was one regrettable area of his past that Ben might have been able to exploit – he was a former cocaine addict. He later said he wished his story had been dealt with more openly on the show as it probably would have helped him rack up the votes.

"They sort of brushed it under the carpet," he rued. *"In fairness to the show, coke addiction isn't really family stuff to talk about at 7pm on a Saturday, I guess. But I was fine with speaking about it because it was something that happened that I'm OK with now.*

"I was pretty honest about it. When the story broke, the show kind of ignored it and let the public make their own minds up, which might have been a good way of doing it but I'm not sure we couldn't have handled it better.

"I was a very strong contender at that point if you look at the percentage of votes I was getting each week, and I think that if we'd played it up a little bit more it would have been more beneficial to me."

It is hard to deny that, regaled by accounts of tragedy and triumph, we feel a little bit more sympathetic and interested in that contestant and their plight. Likeable series five finalist Daniel Evans revealed, in his first audition, how his wife had died. Regardless of his upbeat and entertaining performances, the judges seemed intent on bringing up his loss at every opportunity. *"You were singing that for your wife, weren't you Daniel?"* they asked.

Rightly or wrongly, his loss was brought back to the surface throughout the show. Sometimes this overshadowed his singing abilities – even if *he* didn't mention his dearly departed.

Career consultant Sital Ruparelia, who runs sitalruparelia.com, believes this was something that helped voters understand Daniel and his motivations. *"Based on talent and ability, Daniel Evans, the weaker singer, should have been voted out weeks before he was, but he stayed because he had a personal story that connects with large sections of the target audience.*

"In his first appearance on the show he told how the death of his wife had encouraged him to pursue his dream of singing. Every time he sings, he is singing for her. His willingness to share his story helped the audience connect with him at a personal level – and so a large proportion of the public continued to vote for him – even though he is not the best singer on the show.

"Other singers in the competition also had personal stories, which the audience connect with. Laura White didn't have a story – and so not enough members of the public empathised and connected with her at a personal level to vote in the numbers required to keep in her in.

"In the information-overloaded, time-poor world we live in, stories are what a target audience connects with: authentic stories that resonate with people at an emotional level."

Indeed, although 2008's Bolton belter Laura may have been fantastically gifted, no one knew anything about her to relate to. She was just a very talented jazz singer and that's not necessarily a fun thing to watch on the box, unless they're behaving Winehouseishly. Take note Gabrielle Cilmi and Duffy.

Psychotherapist and author Phillip Hodson says: ***"People need a sense of your identity and where you've come from so that they can be sympathetic towards you and vote to keep you in. People vote with their emotions on shows like The X Factor.***

"Be honest but not overly so and be careful about what you say. You want to share enough so people relate to you but not so much that you feel exposed."

So you don't need to go too personal here, *or* too sad. If you have had a horrible experience, you don't want silly TV writers dismissing it as a sob story. But if you *do* want to share, then leave the big tearjerkers until later on in the competition and hit them right between the eyes with it.

The main requirements of a good story are:

★ Choosing something that people can relate to. Teased at school? Tell, tell, tell. Had a big hairy mole from your face removed that has somehow undermined your dazzling, catalogue-modelling career? Open up. You want to show that although the experience was scarring, you got through it – thanks to your singing – and are now a much stronger person because of it.

The perennially perky Sarah of the swingorilliant Same Difference from series four said at the time that her bullying was prompted by her strong desire to sing and perform. The cool girls at her school in Portsmouth didn't take too kindly to this Disney-esque dream and mercilessly teased the poor mite throughout her time at secondary school.

"I was bullied badly," Sarah recalled. *"There was a group of girls who didn't see me as normal because all I wanted to do was sing. They thought I was weird.*

"I went through absolute hell – I would walk through corridors and have abuse shouted at me. They would hack into my e-mail account and abuse all my friends so they turned against me.

"I would be called names and I was even hit once. It went on from 13 or 14 until I left school at 16. The main reason I left to go to London to theatre school was to get away from them – I didn't want to go to college with them."

Syrupy-sweet Sarah made sure to demonstrate that, despite the horrible teasing at school, she had learned something from the experience. *"I got away from it,"* she said, *"and it made me a stronger person. In some ways I am quite glad it happened. It has really made me appreciate stuff like this."*

Hurrah. We can sympathise till the cows come home but we still want a tidy ending.

★ TIP: If you were bullied at school, you might want to mention that it's the instigators whom you now pity, not yourself.

★ Don't choose a rubbish story.

Alisha Bennett from series four blubbed that she was out on a limb in the competition because she was the oldest girl. Alisha was 23 at the time she was in the show. TWENTY-THREE! It's not like she was being mugged for her pension book or fitted for incontinence pants.

Even more pitifully, Scott Bruton from series five could only muster up that he'd left his job as a Pontin's Bluecoat to be taken seriously after Simon Cowell initially sniggered at his family entertainment credentials.
"I had to quit my job," he mourned in *The Mirror*. *"It was Pontin's or* The X Factor *and I had to look at what, hopefully, was best for me in the long run. I have put a lot at risk."*

If in doubt, say nowt.

★ Stories about appearance where we can see the physical progress usually go down well.

Edinburgh lass Lisa Milbury from 2008 appeared to have won over the judges when she told them about her incredible 18-stone weight loss, which earned her the title of Scottish Slimmer of the Year. She showed pictures of herself before and after, illustrating that such a transformation *is* possible. Which is a nice thing to hear when you're lying on the couch swamped in chocolate wrappers watching the show.

★ Bereavement Is something that can hardly fail to win people over. Let's put cynicism to one side here. It's a hideous experience that almost everyone has to go through at some time in their lives and we can quite clearly understand why the hopefuls are saddened by their loss. If the person who died happened to be the one person who believed in you the most, then so be it. Not many people would wish death on their relatives and loved ones to scoop up the *X Factor* crown.

Polesworth dinner-lady Niki Evans felt the wrath of the blogs in 2007. They suggested she was talking about her dead father – who had secretly got the *X Factor* audition forms in his drawers to send off for Niki as a surprise – to gain sympathy from the public. The wronged warbler had to heartbreakingly defend herself and, afterwards, almost had to prove that she would rather have her dad alive than be on the talent show.

Niki told *The Sunday Mercury*: **"Dad dying wasn't a sob story, it was a real thing that happened to me.**

"I actually hadn't told anyone about how I came to audition. But my mum had let it slip that I found the X Factor application form in my dad's stuff."

2008 singer Daniel Evans also attracted the fury of viewers for seemingly skating through the rounds because his wife – and mother of his toddler daughter – died two years beforehand.

They suggested that he banged on about his loss – when, in reality, the dad-of-three had only mentioned it at the audition because he'd been asked why he'd applied (his wife had always encouraged him to give singing a shot). Daniel dedicated a song to his wife when he found himself in the bottom two – but other contestants have dedicated songs to departed loved ones from their past too. Sharing his experience might have helped people understand him and it certainly helped people put themselves in his shoes. However, he also won fans for having fun on stage and for being the type of singer that many mums and ladies of a certain age would like.

★ TIP: Assert that you don't want to just be known for your bereavement.

"I want The X Factor *to be about me and my singing,"* Daniel announced on the show. *"I don't want to be seen as the sob-story guy. I look for the good things in every situation. My wife was always the first person to say, 'It could be worse'. And she was right. I have a beautiful daughter. We had ten wonderful years together. Things could certainly be better. But they could also be a whole lot worse."*

So, mention your bereavement if you want to but be prepared for people suggesting, perhaps unfairly, that you're milking it.

★ Give evidence of an incident that almost stood in the way of your singing.

Spaniard Ruth Lorenzo moved to the USA when she was 10. At a mere 13, she had to start burger flipping to earn more money for her poor family. Ruth's fast-food duties meant she was falling back in schoolwork and, as a result, was at risk of being kicked out of a choir that was classed as an extracurricular activity.

The put-upon warbler had already been asked to leave the swimming squad and been banned from the junior prom in an effort to free up more hours to burn the midnight oil studying.

"Thirteen is young to be working," she admitted on the show, *"but I've always been a big girl. I was the size I am now at 11. People never thought I was underage. So no one found out.*

"In the US you have to get good grades in your subjects to be allowed to do the extracurricular after-school clubs, but my grades were poor because I was working so hard. I begged them, 'I am doing my best I can just now. Just please don't kick me out of my singing class.' I am very grateful for how kind and loving they were towards me and that they let me stay in the singing class."

★ Don't bring out your full story until you get through to Boot Camp, otherwise you've just opened a whole tin of worms without actually gaining a place in *The X Factor*. You want to eke out bits and bobs throughout the series so that people have an ongoing reason to be interested in you. (Continue to do this if you become a proper pop star. If you're gay, be enticingly ambiguous until you've got everyone on side. If you use drugs, be outrageously coy on the subject until you're busted, then sell your rehab pictures. If you don't actually sing or play on your CDs, be a good dancer. And so on.)

"You've got to know how to work the media," confirms Ben Mills. *"Simon Cowell is very good at that, he's very smart. You have to work it to your advantage in* The X Factor *and be prepared to talk about your past."*

★ Be prepared to be met with sceptics and have an answer for them if they moan about your story. If you have been through a horrible experience, don't let them get the better of you.

As teacher Beverley Trotman, from series four, protested: *"These things we say aren't sob stories. They're real life; they're things that have happened to us. They're what have driven us here. I can't help that."*

★ If your story isn't too wretched, then you might want to go back to the scene of the boo-boo and cry a lot when you get there. Now might be a good time to mention that you're "a fighter who won't give up". Wear a roll-neck jumper while you do that – you want to show your serious side.

★ If you can, get the production company to splice a montage of you as a sprog with the music of Enya or 'You Raise Me Up' on in the background.

★ Be reunited with an old family member and muffle

phrases of delight at seeing them again into their shoulder as you hug them.

★ Don't cry *all the time*. It can be off-putting, so stick with just once an episode if you can – or at least just once an episode about your traumatic experience.

Same Difference staged a masterclass of timing when they followed a performance of S Club 7's 'Never Had A Dream Come True' with Sarah's tearful revelation of her school years bullying. The sobbing was most effective because the exuberant hopeful had, up to that point, been a bundle of happy energy, never letting a frown darken her sunny face. Even non-believers were swayed when they learned what she'd been through at school. Inspired.

"I knew that Sarah was keen to sing it," observed Simon Cowell, *"and it obviously had some memories for her. We have always only seen one side to Same Difference so it was important to show a different one. Who knows whether it helped them get through? That wasn't necessarily the point of it. It certainly wasn't the only sob story on the show."*

★ Deny all existence of having a sob story. If you have no tear-jerking tales to tell, why not try a different tactic and mark yourself out as someone who is completely normal and who just wants to be known for his/her singing? Then again, if you opt for this risky strategy you could end up like Rhydian who told *The Sun*: "I've no sob story like some of the contestants, so they make me look arrogant instead. I hate myself when I watch the show."

Here's a few stories you might want to take up in case you're stuck for a few ideas. You might also want to check out *Peter Kay's Britain's Got The Pop Factor...* for a few ideas too.

★ An ex-soldier who fought in a recent or still-in-the-news campaign (Iraq, Afghanistan) was wounded everywhere except his/her throat.

★ Someone who was told they couldn't sing at school, and who was kicked out of the school choir and remarkably learned how to sing like an angel.

★ Someone who was banned from listening to music by super-strict music-hating parents and yet managed to reach adulthood blessed with an outstanding singing talent.

★ Someone whose throat was badly damaged and had to have a throat replacement and can only communicate in song.

★ A reformed bully who wants to right their wrongs by singing for the world.

So, take a deep breath and tell all.

HOW TO WIN X FACTOR

chapter eight

TIME TO START CRYING

"This means so much to me."

It's a small wonder *The X Factor* isn't sponsored by Kleenex, considering the number of times the contestants reach for the hankies and break down into shuddering fits of blubbering before our very eyes. But let's not forget that this is a trying time for our vocal prodigies of the future.

They had their dreams and talent affirmed by the likes of Cowell ("You know what, I like you") and co ("That's a yes from me", "That's a double yes with bells on top from me") after years of belting out the hits of Whitney Houston in their local to an audience of one drunken heckler and a flatulent dog. Now, the great British public likes them; really likes them. Well, for two weeks anyway.

Even series five crooner Daniel Evans said he found the timed tearjerkers a bit hard to stomach before he entered the show.

Daniel told Unreality TV: *"I used to watch the show years back and wonder what they were getting so emotional about. I mean, they sing for two minutes, then they go back to their big house. Now I know it's non-stop: it's filming, it's choreography, it's vocal coaching. It's intense."*

And intense it looks from the sofa. You can see the beads of sweat drying out on the contestants' foreheads as they realise they are liked because they are real and genuine and consequently, through the medium of popular Saturday night television, have finally accepted who they are. And, every week, when viewers pick up the phone to vote for them, it's because they like them for being real and genuine and for having all this thus far unrecognised talent. When our dear contestants sit back in front of the camera and contemplate such great acceptance and popularity, the years of being unrecognised catch up with them and it all comes flooding out again.

Flood being the operative word here because, my, don't those tears roll thick and fast. It all comes back. Hang on, what did the kids used to call them again? Wasn't it Eggy on account of the egg-cress sandwiches mum made *once* for lunch in secondary school? Yes, yes it was. So they sagely tell the camera crew, between sobs, about the terrible time they had trying to get a girlfriend – let alone getting their talent noticed, apart from one dear old teacher who'll be mentioned at a later date – at school with the nickname "Eggy". And then something catches their eye. It's a newspaper. They're on it – Eggy's on it – as a pimply teen dressed up as Katie Brown in the school production of *Calamity Jane*. Hayley Jenkins from the upper sixth is on record as saying that Eggy had fought for the best costumes and made the leading lady break down once after stealing her hat. It's. All. Getting. A. Bit. Much.

Remember loveable former cross-dressing reality TV stalwart Austin Drage's tears as he realised he'd finally been accepted by people and, most of all, himself? Remember the interviews he gave about his school days, accompanied by pictures of him as a bespectacled teen? He no longer had to compete in late night Channel 4 shows like *Boys Will Be Girls* where he had to try to convince people he was a lady to climb pop's greasy pole. He could just sing songs and have his hair ruffled by Cheryl Cole and he was accepted. But with great acceptance comes great bouts of crying. Poor Austin threatened to erode his face away with his monsoons of tears, his lower lip permanently puckered and at the ready for a fresh epiphany. He was liked. He was accepted. He was on *The X Factor.*

Austin, dubbed "sobbing Austin" in the press, told Digital Spy: *"I'm emotional but I'm not ashamed of that fact.*

"It's not like I'm miserable all the time. Nine out of ten times I'm quite happy. I'm not afraid to get emotional about my music because I love what I do. If people see me crying because I love what I do, I don't see that as a particularly bad thing."

After a good hearty sob, our contestants have just enough composure to plaster foundation over their artfully reddened eyes and whip out a new handy 10-pack of tissues. Then it's time to meet their idol – the idol they've been dreaming of meeting since they were nippers – and the sobs start again.

"I can't believe it," gulped Alexandra Burke on meeting American pop booty shaker Beyoncé on the show. But rather than pinch herself, she cried herself back to reality. *"I've been ... dreaming ... dreaming.... about this for... so... so .... long,"* came choked sentences of gushed admiration. (Four months later, she posted on Twitter: *"Oh my GOD I just met Beyoncé AGAIN!! And this time I didn't cry!!" Bless.)*

Crying for joy is such a momentary release for our poor pop potentials that they have to bring themselves crashing back down to earth with a filmed call to their families. The call has the bonus of showing that they haven't lost their roots despite their huge "journey". The call is every contestant's trump card. They might have been living away from home for 17 years. They may only get in touch with their family once every six months. They may not even *like* their family. But as soon as the family have picked up the phone and established that it's their very popular relative from *The X Factor*, you can be sure that the events of the week will spill out and they'll be crying all over again.

Laura White cried her peepers out at interviews the week before the live shows started in series five, so much did she yearn for her hometown of Bolton (whose pop progeny include Danny Jones from McFly).

Laura said: *"I am a bit homesick and I miss my family and all the people up north."*

And all this is before the sobbing contestants have even taken to the stage for the live showdown: an hour and a half of pure, emotionally charged showboating. The judges could shoot down their song – which means a lot to them this week because it was the song they sang for Mrs Davis the music teacher, who was the first person to take note of their talent. With one curl of the lip and cheap shot comment based on your song's title ("'I Will Always Love You' – not with that song I won't"), dreams disintegrate. New hairdos might be called "mumsy", outfits "disgrace to fabric" and voices "pitiful". All hard things to deal with, so it's no wonder they find themselves in tears again.

JLS hunk Aston Merrygold didn't live up to his last name and was in floods after his group found themselves in the bottom two in 2008, with Rachel Hylton, on the Take That-themed week. The crowd-pleasing singer worried that his angelic vocals had landed the band in the unfavourable position and was inconsolable as Cheryl Cole soothed his tears, sympathetically musing that he couldn't carry the whole band and shouldn't feel guilty. If Aston had had the foresight, he would have collapsed at Cheryl's feet, beating his fists on the floor, and snagged a reassuring hug from the Girls Aloud star in the bargain. Must cry harder next time Aston.

Aston's bandmate Ortise Wlliams said at the time: *"When Simon told us last week that we could win the show, it triggered another flood of tears from Aston. He's fragile and often takes the blame on his shoulders, which he shouldn't."*

However, Aston's fans didn't mind the youngster's tears. They flooded fansites and the official ITV page saying how much they were moved by his emotion, and how they wanted to comfort him. The lesson here is, if you're going to cry, make sure your fans feel sorry enough for you to see it as an advantage.

Even better, get a judge to cry for you to show how rocked they were over your performance. Cheryl broke into sobs for good reason when she learned that cuddly 2008 contestant Daniel Evans had come to the audition because his late wife had told him he had a good shot. *"It was like he was singing about his wife,"* wailed the weeping warbler.

On a less heart-wrenching level, judges have been known to break down after particularly powerful performances. Dannii was a tear-stained wreck when Rhydian sang his heart out on *X Factor* favourite 'You Raise Me Up' in 2007's love songs week. *"I can't speak,"* she said, oxymoronically. *"That was so beautiful. I felt you were singing it personally to me. It was just incredible."*

When the singing's over, our plucky hopefuls face an hour's waiting with their equally trembling-lipped fellow contestants and some actors from *Corrie*. The lovely Holly Willoughby puts a fine toothcomb through their performances on ITV2's *The Xtra Factor*, gallantly saying that they were "amazing" and looked like proper pop stars on the stage. If they make it through this nervy hour without crying, it'll undoubtedly be the next instalment that trips them up – the results show. Finding out whether they or their closest friends on the show – which is all of them, of course, because they've grown so close and are just one big happy family – have got through to the next round often induces another tsunami of salty tears.

Just think of Derry teen Eoghan Quigg, who erupted in vast geysers of grief when he learned that close pal Diana Vickers had been given the axe from the show. As Diana sang her final song – Dido's 'White Flag' – Eoghan bolted onto the stage, his eyes crimson and glistening with distress.

"The emotion of the moment got the better of me," Eoghan told *The Daily Mail*, *"and when she was singing her farewell song, I rushed out and gave her a hug.*

"I couldn't hold back the tears. I know a lot of people have called me a crybaby because of it.

"But I'm not ashamed of what I did. I was absolutely gutted for her. For me, it was the hardest moment of The X Factor."

And what about Diana's puffy-eyed breakdown when she was told she couldn't sing on Mariah Carey week because of her laryngitis? The object of Eoghan's affections was seen peering out from beneath a duvet, dressing gown firmly tied, eye make-up artfully done, watching the show. Tears cascaded down her face as she explained how gutted she was to be missing out on meeting Mimi.

In between was footage of the teen breaking down on her to-camera piece, voice shaking. And, in another choice snippet, on her visit to the throat specialist, Di put her head in her hands and sobbed uncontrollably.

"It's so upsetting that you can't do anything to help yourself," she declared. *"It's so disappointing that everyone else got to meet Mariah Carey at the masterclass and I... I... didn't.*

"This is what I've wanted all my life [entirely possible as Mariah issued her first album the year before lil' Di popped out of Mrs Vickers] *and I can't believe my throat might stand in the way of it."*

But how useful is all this sobbing?

"If you are a closed book on The X Factor," says Phillip Hodson, author of How 'Perfect' Is Your Partner?, *"people won't be able to relate to you."*

Think about 2007's unnervingly bouncy brother-and-sister band Same Difference. For some, they were at first hard to understand. Suddenly, midway through the competition, we saw Sarah sitting in the family kitchen. S Club 7's 2000 single 'Never Had A Dream Come True' was playing in the background. Sarah told the cameras how she used to listen to the hit when pupils were cruel to her at school. She cried. The nation was won over and rightly so. But what about her elder brother Sean? With no S Club-fuelled sobs, Sean and his indelible grin were seen as a wee bit odd. Note to Sean: cry next time.

"For contestants on **The X Factor,**" says Phillip, *"the most important thing they can do if they want to get people to like them is to focus on revealing and feeling. They have to reveal a little – but not too much, as that's also dangerous. And they have to show that by revealing, they can feel – and a good way of doing this is by crying.*

"Crying is a dead giveaway if someone is genuine or not. It helps us suss out people.

"If you cry and people decide it's genuine, people tend to feel sympathy for you and that translates into votes. If they can also attribute it to something and relate to what you're crying about, such as a nasty comment from the judges or an embarrassing performance… people are able to sympathise with you, and even cry and feel sorry for you. If they can do that, then they will vote for you."

But there is a point where weeping can be too much for the audience to stomach. Dear Austin's streaming face didn't help him in the end, and he was booted out after tearfully dedicating The Shirelles' 'Will You Love Me Tomorrow' to his mum. Austin's mate Rachel Hylton's crying also proved too much to take for some.
The likeable mum-of-five sobbed that she'd been judged too harshly even though she'd always been honest with the audience about her former drug problem and having had three of her children taken away. In that case, it was

unfortunately more likely that her past problems were too raw for most people watching, and they couldn't relate to her.

So remember to keep your tears prettily glistening on your cheeks – not showering your face – and make sure you are crying about something people can relate to.

★ NB: Once you've reached the point of being able to weep freely on air, you can graduate to Advanced Crying. For this you will need to make your eyes glisten at will and be able to whip out a pack of Handy Andies at any time. Show how caring you are by handing out tissues to other weeping wannabes.

If in doubt, remember these pointers:

★ Cry if you feel genuinely upset or happy even if you're usually satisfied with a wry smile or frown. Never forget that you're on a TV show and that you have to ramp up whatever you do by at least 75%. Remember how dull the ordinary world is if you need reminding why to cry. Cor, isn't it boring having to wait 10 minutes in Sainsbury's to buy some overpriced, tasteless pasta? Isn't it knuckle-draggingly dull having to heave yourself out of bed every morning to go to a job where the main source of joy is a surreptitious mid-day scowl at your thankless boss's back as they leave for another two-hour lunch? Isn't it mind-crushingly mundane having to come home to be faced with bills demanding to be paid when really you should be spending your dough on guitars, mistresses/toyboys and pricey sunglasses? Doesn't that all make you want to collapse into the foetal position and sob big sticky tears? Well, remember that feeling every time any minor grievance rears its head.

★ Cry if the camera's on you and you alone. You might want to start off saying something funny; telling an amusing anecdote to show that you're not the type of person who usually cries. You're usually so strong. Crying in this case is especially good if you've always been the one to hold it together for the rest of the family. The strong, silent one. Well, strong, silent one, *The X Factor* is your stage and that stage welcomes your salty tears.

★ Cry if everyone else is crying to show that you can relate to other people's emotions. They've coped so well with what life's dealt them and have come up against so much. And look – look with your eyes – here they all are. Standing tall and showing how they've coped, with a good old blub. Boo hoo hoo.

★ Get one of the judges to cry for you so that your fans don't feel like wimps for weeping about your emotional rendition of 'I Will Always Love You'. Who couldn't fail to melt at the sight of the ever-lovely Cheryl Cole wiping away delicate tears with a fairy-like hand? Who wouldn't want to comfort her and support the act she cried over?

★ Cry if you find yourself in the bottom two and you sing a song that "means so much" to you. Think of series five contestant Ruth Lorenzo singing Prince's 'Purple Rain' in week two. It was no wonder that Ruth – with her glistening eyes, her hands in her hair and her high-octave blasting – trounced fellow bottom-two dwellers Girlband with their Eternal-esque version of Aerosmith's 'Don't Want To Miss A Thing'.

★ Cry when you see something sad and want to show what a highly evolved and sensitive person you are and how you care about the Big Important Issues of the Day or at least the things people care about. A good time to do this might be if you see an old or stray dog as you rehearse for the coming week's show. Watch it as it sniffs around a bin as you sing 'Puppy Love'. Isn't that sad? Yes, it is. PS: It might even score you points with Simon Cowell, whose voice is on the RSPCA's appeal to stop animal cruelty ("Listen guys...").

Another good time to do this is if a fan meets you (need we add, on camera) in the streets of an indistinct town. Hopefully they'll say something praiseworthy about you and the friend/parent with them will tearfully say how much they love seeing you on the telly. Don't weep until they've passed you by. Then, as the lucky fan is receding into the distance, let your eyes weep gracious tears. You might want to mention that that person is so brave and you couldn't even begin to imagine what they're going through but will be dedicating the song to them just as a small boost.

★ Reveal a little about yourself and then cry about it. If you have nothing to reveal, a good fail-safe crowd pleaser is saying how much you miss your family. Perhaps mention old Great Aunt Gladys, who was the first to believe in your singing ability and who tragically died six months ago, just before you applied to get on the show. She would have been so proud. Would you like a tissue? Go on then.

★ Don't reveal too much all at once. Hold back some stories so you can filter them through on a week-by-week basis.

★ If in doubt, cry.

There, there. That's better.

chapter nine

GIVE THE IMPRESSION OF BEING A GRAFTER

"I'll give you 110%"

Got three jobs, a family of 17 and a regular Tuesday night slot in a working men's club that still allows members to puff away on ciggies inside? Well remember to remind all and sundry about it my friend.

While as a nation we may loathe bigheads, we're very much in favour of those who've worked so darned hard to get where they are today. Be that person if you're in *The X Factor*. Like the humble sob story, you need to mention how you've been buckling down for years to reach the heady position you're in today. People like diligent workers because it puts all their years of backbreaking slog into focus.

And it's not just us back home who want to feel justified, it's the judges too. Come in fresh from a holiday in St Barts, with a phone book full of A&R people who work for your mum or dad at Universal Records, having decided that you only wanted to give this singing lark a go yesterday so that you can meet Holly Willoughby, and it's fair to assume that most people will be put off.

Here, it's not so much about the money – born in Brighton and raised by a property developer dad and ballet dancer mum in leafy Elstree, Simon Cowell came from a comfortable background – but more about showing that you've put in the hours despite your circumstances – be they for the richer or poorer – all because of your burning love of music.

Laura White said at her audition: ***"I can't ever see myself doing the nine-to-five. I'm driven by music and just want to be given the chance to be heard. That's all I've ever really wanted."***

"I think it's important for people to know I worked so hard before the show," Leona Lewis told *The Sun* after a hard day's pop schlep.

"The X Factor *didn't make me. It helped me a lot. I'm grateful I got the opportunity and for all their support, but before that I'd done a lot of work demoing and playing smoky pubs and clubs.*

"A lot of people give you flak for going on a talent show but I'd worked the circuit and worked so hard for years. Since I was so small it's always been my dream to sing."

After dropping in how hard you've worked to get where you are today, you need to mention how much you want it and how every other job and occupation pales into insignificance compared with your beloved singing. But you need to give evidence of having worked at jobs that other people can understand to show that you're down with the people. Shayne Ward worked in a New Look store, Leon Jackson in Gap. Alexandra was a waitress and Leona Lewis a secretary. Likewise, you need to show you aren't damning of the fact that the rest of us won't be able to jet around the world and warble a few ballads to adoring crowds.

If you can give evidence of having worked a standard job but still pursued your singing in your spare time, then people should respect you. After all, who wants a lazybones to gallivant through the process without breaking into a sweat.

Voices With Soul said: *"The X Factor was such hard work. I know it looks easy but you really do put in a lot of graft. You're given days to learn a song, a dance routine, get used to being on a stage and the idea that 12 million people will be watching you at home.*

"Then there's the fact that you're away from home, which is hard to get used to. And if you are in a band, you have the added pressure of making sure you don't let anyone else in the band down.

"It is fun work, but it's hard work all the same."

Again here, you might want to be seen practising scales on camera and wearing your dance kit around the house to show how much effort you've put into your performance. You might want to be seen at some New-Age confidence-instilling class to overcome your stage fright or some laughter therapy group to try and make your wooden performance more lively. We've all seen those hilarious clips of the Spice Girls sweating in their first managers' studio, and Boyzone tanking in front of a chortling TV audience. We might have winced, but we couldn't fault their gumption. So show the lengths you are going to to become the best you can be. *"Fame costs,"* as Debbie Thingummy intoned at the beginning of each episode of early Eighties viewing essential *Fame*, *"and here's where you start paying – in sweat."* Nice. This will demonstrate that you are going to some lengths to become the best you can be.

If you don't look like you've worked hard then you could come across as arrogant, and if you don't think you need to work hard on your act then you might as well not be there. We at home want to see you putting in the time, otherwise it'd make for pretty dull TV.

Perhaps mention how many early nights you've been having to rest your voice and how you haven't stopped to even check your fan mail. Be seen rising at the crack of dawn going for a jog to keep yourself physically ready for the showdown. You might also want to pop a few vitamin tablets to ward off any nasty infections.

And if you're lucky, your mentor and singing coach will both say on the show how much effort you've put into your skit too, just to reinforce what a worthy winner you would be. Having your loved ones also add in a casual sentence or two about how much time you've put in over the years to reach the standard that you're at today won't hurt either, nor will having the landlord/lady of the pub you used to do karaoke in mentioning how you used to help the "stage crew" set up the mic and all. Get them to mention specific things you've worked on that we at home will easily be able to pick up on.

A good example of this is if you've worked doubly hard to learn a dance even though you ordinarily move like a spider on Rollerblades when asked to boogie. Diana Vickers made sure everyone around her noted how many hours she'd put in to her 'Call Me' and 'Girlfriend' dance routines despite not being wholly comfortable with cutting up the dance floor. It paid off with the naysaying judges heaping the praise on her and duly noting the toil she'd put in to remember her routine.

So for now, let them do all the talking. After all, you've done all the hard slog. It's time for your supporters to sweat it out for a bit on your behalf.

Pop idol ... Series four winner Leon Jackson toasts his success
with some Iron Bru and haggis. (DAVE HOGAN/GETTY IMAGES)

Get Rhyd ... Series four runner-up Rhydian Roberts performs in Birmingham in 2009 after selling a whopping 600,000 copies of his debut album. (STEVE THORNE/REDFERNS)

Drage queen ... Series five's Austin Drage and Laura White pose with drag queen Jodie Harsh soon after their bootings in 2008. (JAMES CURLEY/REX FEATURES)

Oh brother ... Popular siblings Sean and Sarah Smith aka Same Difference, who were finalists in series four, perform on Oxford Street in 2008. (DANNY MARTINDALE/GETTY IMAGES)

Sitting pretty ... Judges Dannii Minogue and Cheryl Cole get ready to dish out criticism and praise on the panel in 2008. (KEN MCKAY/REX FEATURES)

Silent Si ... Louis Walsh takes the rare opportunity to silence his judging pal Simon Cowell. (SHOWBIZIRELAND/GETTY IMAGES)

Call me ... Sarah Smith of Same Difference exercises one of many cute hand gestures to endear the public to vote for her in 2007. (KEN MCKAY/REX FEATURES)

Eogh no ... Diana Vickers comforts a distraught Eoghan Quigg who belted onto the stage in a teary breakdown in 2008 after finding out she'd been eliminated from the competition. (KEN MCKAY/REX FEATURES)

Lighting up ... Series five stars Rachel Hylton, Ruth Lorenzo and eventual winner Alexandra Burke switch on the Oxford Street Christmas lights in 2008. (DANNY MARTINDALE/WIREIMAGE)

Boy band ... Series four runners-up JLS hit the big time with their performance at BBC Radio 1's Big Weekend 2009. (ANDY SHEPPARD/REDFERNS)

Daddy croon ... Father and series five wailer Daniel Evans sings his heart out on the show.
(KEN MCKAY/REX FEATURES)

Teen dream ... Series five finalist Eoghan Quigg performs for BBC's Switch.
(MARK ALLAN/WIREIMAGE)

Be my friend ... Winner Alexandra Burke is overwhelmed when mega superstar Beyoncé Knowles graciously pops up to plug her single 'If I Were A Boy' and sing a duet, 'My Own', in the final. (KEN MCKAY/REX FEATURES)

chapter ten

CONTROVERSIES

"I'd like to say sorry to Simon. Sorry to Dermot and sorry to my mum and dad. But most of all I'd like to say sorry to the people back home who voted for me every week. I'm so disappointed in myself."

While you don't want to be an utter plank, it's advisable to veer along the, "Oh, you support Leeds United but are from *Manchester*" style of controversy rather than the more dangerous, "Oh, you're the girl who happy slapped a teenager" line of hullaballoo in *The X Factor*.

Such a scenario had unfortunate repercussions for one contestant – the then 15-year-old Emily Nakanda from series four – who fell foul of the public after the emergence of a video of her launching into an unprovoked attack on a teenage girl in a "happy slap" prank. Emily, who'd previously melted the hearts of many by recalling the time she nearly died after contracting the vicious stomach infection peritonitis, had to withdraw from the show as the story broke, giving her mum the thankless task of apologising for the teen's bad behaviour.

"As a family we are heartbroken and are very disappointed with Emily's behaviour," announced her mum.

"We feel that there is no choice but to withdraw Emily from the competition. Emily and all the family sincerely apologise to Anna [the victim], her school and all the fans that have supported Emily. Emily regrets her actions but there is no way, as a family, we can excuse her behaviour.

"Emily is very sorry to have let the show, Sharon [Osbourne] and the viewers down."

Rachel Hylton from series five thought she'd escaped the furious storm of controversy when she told the judges in her first audition that she was a reformed drug addict, who tragically had three of her five children taken away from her. The poor Londoner seemed more sinned against than sinning when the hoo-ha followed her around like a bad smell, leading her to beg the public to give her another chance. However, after being spared the axe, the rather too honest mum pumped her hands into the air in a gun salute – promptly incurring the wrath of viewers who thought the gesture distasteful. Ironically, Futureproof, Nicholas Dorsett, Addictiv Ladies and 4Tune had all done the same thing without any comeuppance.

"A lot of black African people and West Indian people do that," protested Rachel to the *News Of The World*. *"It's like when white people do devil's horns and go 'Rock out'. It's the same thing when we go 'Bang, bang, bang'. I'm sorry it's a gun sign but that's how we express ourselves."*

Nevertheless, Rachel's resolute attitude earned her plenty of brownie points when her mentor, Dannii Minogue, crossed swords with Louis Walsh when both wanted their act – Louis' being Croydon boys JLS – to sing the same song.

Yes, the two judges came to verbal blows and caused uproar when they tussled over who should sing 'Rule The World' on Take That week. A live-on-air argument led Dannii to blub immaculate tears. Indeed, so choked was the other Minogue sister that she could barely introduce Rachel to the stage. In a faltering voice, Dannii told everyone back home that she hadn't nicked JLS's song in the first place.

Throughout this hoo and, furthermore, ha, one person stood sensible, calm and strong. Yes indeed. Welcome back to the competition Rachel.

OK, in actuality 27-year-old Rachel was booted out that very same night after a sing-off with JLS. But the point is that in the midst of Louis and Dannii's controversial tantrums, the defiantly calm Rachel looked a shining example of a reasonable adult; one unaffected by the diva-ish antics of others, and who wouldn't morph into one herself.

"I feel sorry for Dannii," said Rachel benevolently. *"It's not her fault."*

When in doubt, follow these rules:

★ It's useful to have a minor controversy to keep people interested in you and show off a new side to your personality. You want to show that you're utterly adept at dealing with the onslaught of fame, even if it means people knowing all about that time you wet yourself in a Sainsbury's car park aged 28 and that privately you are a seething mass of bitterness for that story and the CCTV footage being unearthed and sent as a round-robin to every office in the country.

★ Minor controversies are much less personally damaging. Been given the week off sick from the show but been granted immediate entry to the next round, à la Diana Vickers? It'll raise a few eyebrows without incurring the wrath of *The Daily Mail* in the way it would if you confessed to a former crack addiction. (However, these more epic controversies can certainly stir up interest. If in doubt, go small and elaborate more as the weeks go on.)

★ It's always good to banter with the judges – it makes the show entertaining – but make sure you don't cross the mark. You don't want to come across as too bolshy or disrespectful. You *will* have to change aspects of your act – whether that's style, song choices or the way you clomp about the stage – because, otherwise, the judges would be out of a job (and do you want to be the one who consigns Dannii to a life on the pantomime circuit?). Just make sure you do a Rachel Hylton and take the comments "on board" rather than dismiss them outright.

"You need to be open to suggestion," says Peter Robinson of cult music website Popjustice. *"You have to accept that every single person in the Top 10 has had to make compromises to be where they are today, and that you as an* X Factor *contestant will too – and probably more so.*

"If you have too much personality, people won't like you, and if you are too controversial, people won't like you. There's only so many times you can answer back to a judge as Will Young did on Pop Idol *before people get bored of watching it and find it rude. So you need to toe the line."*

Series four contestant Daniel de Bourg concurs: *"Even if you don't agree with what the judges said – and you won't always – you need to respect them*

"On my final week, I sang 'Build Me Up Buttercup', which wasn't right for me. But it would have been disrespectful of me to stand there slagging it off because my mentor [Louis] did their best by me.

"You have to respect what they have to say and not argue too much. At the end of the day, it's an entertainment show and you're there to enjoy it as much as you are to compete in it. So there's no need getting worked up about it."

So how can you handle any rude remarks from the judges without being too aggressive – or, at the end of the spectrum, passive?

Phillip Hodson says: *"The best way to cope with insults in The X Factor is to carry on as though nothing has happened. If you try to deflect the insults, you are endowing them with power by bothering... unless you are Dorothy Parker, of course, and can destroy your critics with instant verbal vehemence."*

★ If you have had a racy past life always admit your faults and show what a changed person you are. It's usually best to do this while filming a moody to-camera piece, soundtracked by a Snow Patrol song with an upward key change. That key change is the time to talk about the changes that *you've* made in your life. Show pictures of yourself looking a bit wan or grumpy, even if you had a jolly good time during those dark years. Talk through the "pain" that the controversy caused your loved ones. It might also be useful to look straight at the camera and say, "Sorry, can we stop this now?" and then peg it off.

Series four's girl group Hope were shorn of member Sisi Jghalef when it was discovered she had a criminal conviction. The band carried on valiantly through the tears (to be kicked out later in the live showdown). They said how sorry they were that she'd left at the time but made it clear that they weren't involved. Take your lead from their example and maintain pristine behaviour, whatever mishaps your rivals, relatives or bandmates are getting into. Shayne Ward showed what a thoroughly rounded chap he is despite his dad's well-publicised misdemeanours. Not that every potential contestant should get loved ones to commit crimes... but if you can triumph against weighty odds then it's fair to say that most people will respect you for it.

Another great way of getting the coverage and attention through controversy, without embarrassing revelations from a vengeful ex or a family member doing time, is by having a voting scandal. Did ITV flash up the wrong number for fans to vote for you for all of five seconds, as they did with Ruth Lorenzo? Milk that sucker. Did some electronic glitch mean that people at home had trouble voting for you the week that you were in the bottom two? Get them to complain. The good thing about a voting scandal is that you'll look like the wronged party against the faceless big company. And, thanks to several high-profile vote fiascos, people will be on the lookout for it and it'll be picked up by the press.

Take Laura White's "shock" exit from the competition in week five. Some 50,000 fans of the former favourite besieged media watchdog Ofcom with complaints that they couldn't get through, leading to rumblings about whether the Bolton lass was unlawfully booted. Even the government's Culture Secretary, Andy Burnham, put in his two penneth worth, saying how unfair it was that the "wonderful" singer had been given the heave-ho. Previous winner Leona Lewis declared she was "outraged" and even rent-a-gob Lily Allen announced she was narked by the result.

Laura Reading, who put the seething petition online, said: *"There must be an official inquiry into what has gone on. It's a disgrace."*

To the fury of campaigners, Louis Walsh replied: *"Laura was in the bottom two – her performance was bad and her styling was even worse. She didn't get the public support and got three votes from the judges. No one in the bottom two ever wins* The X Factor. *That's just a fact. Laura was never going to win."*

In the end, Ofcom ruled that there had been no wrongdoing on ITV's part. Despite the outcome, the controversy proved useful for Laura. Previously, *The Sun* had quoted a source as saying that *"some people were bitching about the relationship"* she had with Matthew Firsht, who organises audiences for *The X Factor* and other shows through his company Applause Store – but presumably those people were silenced by Laura's *X Factor* exile (although the paper also noted that *X Factor* spokespeople said they had no problem with the romance). She might have been booted, but at least Laura had the ego-massaging bonus of fans rallying around her and fighting her corner.

THE AMOUR CARD

Maybe Laura should have played the amour card like competition comrades Diana Vickers and Eoghan Quigg.

The teens were said to be in a romantic relationship (though far be it for anyone to suggest that it might have been unusual if two cute teens who spent every day together did not start to fancy each other a little bit). Their gentle teasing and hair-pulling warmed the cockles of our hearts and we forgot for a bit that, at the time, Diana had a boyfriend and that if she and Eoghan were smitten – something they both denied – we don't like cheats.

Regardless of that and the annoyance it might have caused Diana and Eoghan, the speculation did no harm in raising the soppy singers' profiles and keeping interest levels in them high.

★ The lesson here is that a suggested fling is a good way of gaining a little publicity so long as it is with another contestant and – important this – of the hand-holding variety only.

PREVIOUS EXPERIENCE

If you've previously had record contracts and put out singles, you might want to reveal these once you're in the final 12. Play them down and laugh them off. Oh, how terrible you were back then. Did you really put a glockenspiel on that single? Did you really think those Spliffy jeans and Naf Naf jacket looked good? Viewers will generally tolerate failed pop stars on *Celebrity Love Island* but might look unfavourably on chancers looking to give their stumbling career a leg-up. Remember the howls of outrage that greeted the appointment of Lisa Scott-Lee's husband, Johnny Shentall, to *Popstars* band Hear'Say? He'd not made the big time as part of Boom! – remarkable given their splendid name – and, thanks to the public perception of "a fix", he wouldn't find lasting fame this way either.

Series four contestant Daniel de Bourg said: *"I was pretty upfront about my past as a songwriter. I had nothing to hide.*

"I wasn't boastful about it, but I didn't want anyone to think that I'd only been put through because I'd written

for Jamelia [2000's Top Five hit 'Money']. But, having worked with recording artists, it did help when I went into the studios and knew a little bit about arranging a song."

Likewise, series two's Maria Lawson was quick to stress the difference between being a solo contestant on *The X Factor* and being a backing singer for Gabrielle. *"But,"* she admitted, *"the experience I'd had did make it easier for me to get used to singing in front of such a large crowd. Still, nothing prepared me for performing in front of 10 million people every week!"*

The main thing to remember with controversies in *The X Factor* is that providing they're not too awful you can fix most of them by saying how sorry you are and measuring them against your current life. If you say how much you've changed and how this is your chance to put right the wrongs you did, you should be quids in. Repentance is Good.

Take a deep breath, apologise, and let the votes for you flood in.

HOW TO WIN X FACTOR

chapter eleven

BE SO VERY HUMBLE... BUT HAVE PASSION, PASSION, PASSION

"I can't believe this is happening to me."

Considering their musical merits, *X Factor* contestants are notoriously modest about their achievements.

"I never thought I'd even get through the auditions," they all say, bewildered that someone has recognised that they don't sound like a strangled cat. "I can't believe this is happening to me."

And in fairness to the humble bunch, being arrogant never really goes down well on the telly, so why would they bother banging on about how great they think they are? We want the contestants to be quietly confident of their talents. You know, kind of like they've been told by a few people at the local karaoke that they can hold a note, believed them and thought they'd try out at the auditions, and if they didn't get through then they'd forget about their pop star aspirations. But, hey, they had to just give it this one last shot – even if they are serial auditionees – and try out because otherwise they'd be on their deathbed in decades' time thinking, "What if? What if I had performed my version of 'Without You' in front of Simon Cowell and he had *liked* it and I won *The X Factor* and brought out three albums and occasionally presented the *National Lottery Jet Set* show on a Saturday night? What if?"

But luckily for the contestants, "What if?" won't be bugging them in years to come, because they have given it a shot and have remained oh so grounded with it all. After all, we want them to feel grateful that we've deemed them good enough to have bagged our vote.

Maria Lawson says: ***"Simon hates ego.***

"He likes humble people and so do the other judges and the public for that matter.

"You can let yourself shine in the live shows without being too arrogant. You don't have to hold back but just don't be too pushy, because it doesn't wash. Between them the judges have worked with some of the biggest pop stars in the world and they're not going to appreciate you being too up yourself.

"You can still be quietly confident in your abilities and say to them, 'I am what you're looking for' without being too boastful.

"Just be nice and courteous and if you have any problems with them, raise them in a polite way, because the judges haven't got time for ego or drama."

★ So keep telling everyone how shocked you are that you're in the competition, that you're amazed you got through to the live rounds and that you expect to go home every week.

★ If this isn't working, a blinder to play is to whip out a picture of you with one of the judges before you were famous. Hopefully you'll look a bit gawky in the picture too, so people can see how much you've "bettered" your life through the power of the telly but remained gracious. Then you can shove it in front of the camera and say, "A year ago I was queueing up to get Simon Cowell to scribble on the first page of my Simon Cowell biography and now look – a year later and I am going to his birthday parties and everything. I can't believe it!"

This will hopefully give floating voters the incentive to vote for you, because they might also want to be invited to the disapproving judge's house and they might feel that because you've done it – you who up until last year still wore purple polyester shell suits – then so can they.

Try not to sound too down on yourself, because although the great British public are a kind and generous lot, we don't want to have to listen to your existential crisis every week. Maybe one week in three will do. You might want to try out your endearing modesty with a good dollop of passion. After all, we want you to want to be there and want to win *The X Factor*. But just do it in an unassuming manner.

★ Passion is a major buzz word on *The X Factor*, if not *the* buzz word. So on the other side of the *X Factor* scales, you need to lay down a bag of "passion" that is equal in weight to your bag of "modesty". In this way you become the perfectly balanced TV star.

If our poor contestants forget to join their mitts in a prayer sign or make phone signals with their hands to encourage viewers to vote for them, then we might feel that they're too sure of themselves and reckon they'll fly through the rounds and scoop the prize. Even if they don't.

★ You need to make sure that you show that you're passionate enough about singing and wanting to entertain, but humble enough to say that it won't happen to you (even though there's a good chance it will).

Daniel de Bourg said: *"The way to get on in* **The X Factor** *is to stay as grounded as you possibly can.*

"I did this by treating everyone around me the same and keeping in touch with my loved ones, who would always bring me down a peg or two if I ever got above my station. If not, you'll soon lose those friends and respect and the judges won't like you."

Exactly. So grovel away and wheedle on about how grateful you are for your chance to live your passion. Sorted.

chapter twelve

DON'T BE TOO QUIRKY... BUT DON'T BE TOO DULL EITHER

"Who does she think she is!?"

Who would have thought that by going bare-footed and curling her hands around her face, Diana Vickers would have attracted the wrath of so many haters in 2008? But anything is possible on *The X Factor,* and sometimes the decision to whip off the trainers and parade your tootsies around stage is off-putting for people back home.

"Who does she think she is?" we thought. Kicking off her clodhoppers and strolling around that stage like she owns the place while the rest of them have to keep their shoes and socks on? Wafting her tootsies on the telly like some brazen hippy. Tsk. And what about those hands of hers that she swept around her face like she was performing or something?

The hands that when raised to her cute-as-a-button face formed into a "claw"? Doesn't she know The Rules? Doesn't she know that no one on talent contests had done that ever? As a result of this alarming outburst, the poor blonde teen found herself the subject of several Facebook groups set to wrong the rights of her overactive hands and bare feet.

One Diana disser said: *"Yes, you have a hand, yes, you have a face, but you don't need to caress it every week."*

Another added: *"She has a very cute voice and is quite quirky, but watching her is very, very irritating."*

The northern teen took the barrage of insults pretty well and managed to laugh them off. Later, she conceded that she might have been a little too kooky for *The X Factor*: *"I definitely think I am different – but* The X Factor *was a really, really good thing for me to do."*

Diana told Digital Spy: *"The claw thing did make me a bit self-conscious and I tried to tame it.*

"Brian Friedman [our choreographer] would say to me, 'Tut tut Diana, the claw's coming back'. When it started rising to my face I'd be like, 'Oh no!' But if I stood there like a wooden spoon and never did anything with my arm, people would be like, 'Why does this girl never move?'"

Quite. The bare-footed *X Factor* princess even conceded that toeing the line with her footwear and attitude would have meant losing the respect of those around her.

"Some people have such a problem with me, I am like a magnet to it all," sighed Diana. *"But I would rather people*

adore me or despise me than go, 'She's all right', as that's boring."

But while Diana was admirable in her defiance to stay sweetly different from the rest of her *X Factor* alumni, showing too many sides to your personality can be a confusing thing for us back home.

"Stereotypes are established very quickly," says Phillip Hodson. *"This is the nice, thin one. This is the jolly, fat one. The fact that you can be more than one stereotype is sometimes hard for people to comprehend.*

"They might not want you to appear on one radio show and be funny and opinionated and then go on a TV show later that day and be quiet. We all like to label people and put them in their slots because it makes them easier for us to understand and deal with."

Poor Diana had at first come across as a sweet 17-year-old who could only make contented little hums of excitement in answer to the judges' praise. Now she was some conceited little madam – despite saying absolutely nothing to suggest this – and we were all too busy getting peeved by her hands and feet to take note of her singing.

Ultimately, it was a few samey songs that earned Diana the boot, but the wheels of motion started turning when she dared to be a little too different.

And what about Rhydian Roberts from series four? An opera singer who didn't appear to smarm up with his fellow contestants in front of the cameras, he was immediately classified as "ruthless" and monstrous – largely because, whenever he was on the screens, the doom-laden 'Phantom Of The Opera' was playing behind him.

Rhydian sang opera. Opera! And he seemed unswayable in his self-confidence. He'd also been trained to sing and the like by the Birmingham Conservatoire, so probably thought the daily practices were a walk in the park. And, to top it off, Rhydian announced that he didn't believe in sex before marriage. Though far be it for anyone to suggest that this was probably because no one had yet wanted to have sex with someone whose strange white quiff made him look like an extra from *Star Trek*.

The Rhyddler also came out each week, face set determined to win – and upfront in his desire to do so (a huge quirk in *The X Factor*) – with songs that were markedly different from the usual Whitney covers. *West Side Story* one week, *Phantom Of The Opera* the next.

A cover of synth-pop duo the Pet Shop Boys' 'Go West' – first recorded by New York gay icons The Village People – signalled a change in the chat about the Rhyddler. Maybe it was the sailor costumes. Maybe it was the eye-grabbing background singers. Who knows, but Rhydian had changed from being arrogant and odd – a title he scarcely deserved – to being funny old Rhyddler.

Prior to this, Rhydian had set about his message of change with a fantastic cover of pop-punk Pink's 'Get

The Party Started' and followed it through with a series of performances that thrilled and entertained us at home and led to a nation being thoroughly won over.

Lively Kimberley Southwick from series four was labelled as bonkers during her first audition, having joyously skipped through her auditions, full of energy and banter. The endearing motormouth was similarly energetic throughout Boot Camp and the live finals. But while some saw Kimberley's youthful, non-stop chattering as charming, others found her a little too extroverted and kooky for her own good.

Later, country-and-western fan Kimberley conceded that her over-the-top verbosity might have been off-putting for voters back home. *"The way they've edited everything makes me look 10 times more loopy than I was at any one moment in time!"* she trilled to Digital Spy. *"Some people have found me annoying, but I've found myself annoying when I've watched it back, so that's just the way it goes. I was me the whole way along, so I'm not really fussed about it."*

While we're here, we might as well mention the king of quirk: Chico Slimani. Not only was he the underdog (which, as we'll find out later, is a good thing), he was also kooky. He utterly believed in himself and his abilities. Now, although quiet self-confidence is appreciated, outright belief usually comes back to bite contestants on the backside. Chico danced in a way that lacked any self-consciousness. He chatted up women before his audition, even kissing some. He told Simon that he *"couldn't be compared to anybody"* and broke into a throat-curdling rendition of Prince's 'Kiss' in his audition.

Chico told *Metro*: *"There were people who could sing better than me in my series but nobody else did what I did.*

"People said to me: 'You're not the best singer' but they didn't tell the other contestants: 'You're not the best entertainer.' It's swings and roundabouts. If you want to have a laugh and not take things too seriously, then I'm your man. If you want the hairs on your neck to stand up, then listen to [felow contestant] Andy Williams."

Fortunately for Senor Slimani, 2005 judge Sharon Osbourne loved him. He, in return, was typically charming, telling the famous wife and mum that she looked lovely. Simon Cowell, who initially walked out of Chico's audition after Louis and Sharon voted for him, came round and called him a "natural entertainer" – but it took a long time for his kinks to be straightened out. In the end, Chico tried the self-mocking route with a catchphrase-come-song 'It's Chico Time', which knocked Madonna off the number one spot, and a cute troupe of young 'Chicettes' to win over any dissenters back at home, which finally got our seal of approval. But it took a long time and, by the time Chico left the competition three weeks before the final, the joke had worn a little too thin.

And while the former stripper has forged a dubious claim for the nation's affection – bolstered by his post-*X Factor* anti-size-zero song 'Curvy Cola Bottle Body' and a role in

Ricky Gervais' *Extras* – it's probably fair to say that there won't be another contestant like Chico. And if there was, it's unlikely he or she would go as far as the enthralling oddball did.

The point is that although we don't want a big wimp winning the show, we don't want someone too avant-garde triumphing either. They start off whipping their shoes off and what next? We want someone malleable and nice. We want someone a shade duller than ourselves to win so that we know if we had his or her singing talent, we'd go further still as we have the personality too.

"Popularity," says Phillip Hodson, *"requires you either fit in and support and 'mirror' the opinions and values of your peer group, or you make yourself attractively different and persuade the group to abandon their old views and come over to your side.*

"Humour helps, being beautiful helps, but being brilliant at sales is the best gift. Charismatic leaders cause conversions; even dodgy ones like Tony Blair and Bill Clinton.

"If you don't fit in at all, it's time to go and find a new group, but there are always occasions when any of us needs to keep schtum, bite our tongues and not reveal our complete disagreement with some current fad.

"If everyone seems to 'love' the Queen, then don't abuse the monarch to their faces. Kooky only works if the group is

117

broad-minded already – and admires flamboyant individualism."

Too right. And while we probably weren't ready for claws and tootsies on stage, we're also not happy for someone too ordinary to win the show.

In the end, it was being thus that went against soulful non-diva Laura White from series five. Her inoffensive behaviour was soon picked up on by Simon Cowell, who suggested that the perfectly pretty songbird needed a new look because she didn't stand out enough. Unfortunately for Laura, who was initially praised by Simon for having a "lack of image", there can only be a certain number of dullards in the top 12 finalists or else it'd be a bore Olympics for the rest of us back home. It'd be Big Brother four all over again and no one wants that.

Lovely Laura might have had an outstanding voice, good looks and a nice manner, but she had nothing to mark herself out as something new and interesting. Alex had all those things but she was also effervescently bubbly, showing emotion when she was happy instead of being too modest about everything. And Alex had A Point To Prove. Ruth was passionate and Spanish. Diana had an unusual voice and had her overplayed friendship with Eoghan. Dear Laura, as nice as she seemed, didn't show any of her personality despite being a bright and sprightly young thing. So instead, she was the dull "one to beat".

Image consultants Penny Sloane and Debbie Grays say: *"With little Diana last year, the stylists played up her* quirkiness and found outfits that conveyed that kookiness, but that kookiness was always there, it wasn't something they decided to make her be.

"But with Laura, they never quite found her style and she looked uncomfortable."

Career expert Sital Ruparelia, who regularly gives careers advice on BBC radio, says: "Simon Cowell had told Laura that she had something missing – that she needed to work on her image. He was right.

"But it wasn't just about how she looked – her overall personal brand was not distinct, not clear and so, despite her amazing singing ability, she did not have wide appeal."

Evidently, there's a fine line between non-quirky and plain dull. Leona Lewis might be amazingly beautiful with the best singing voice to come out of The X Factor, but she didn't exactly scream interesting in her to-camera pieces. Nor do the cutesy Leon Jackson or Shayne Ward. But the fact is that boring works for The X Factor, provided you give your voting public enough fodder to keep them interested in you.

"Leona Lewis doesn't have much of an X Factor," says Popjustice editor Peter Robinson. "The things that are good about her are really easily definable. But with some people, you can make them into pop stars and Leona had that. Eoghan Quigg from series five however, was never going to be a pop star."

Nice as Leona and all those other *X Factor* winners were, they were all pretty vanilla in their manner and behaviour. What do they miss about being away from home? Their mum's roast dinner. Who doesn't? What are they looking forward to most about their day off? Watching *EastEnders*. Quelle surprise. What's their dream day? Nothing too fancy, a light buffet, their loved ones and a viewing of *The Sound Of Music.* Sorry, did you just hear that noise? Was that the sound of the boring alarm? Yes it was.

Even series three vocal coach Mark Hudson commented that Leona might need some more sparkle to win people over.

Mark said at the time: ***"Leona's voice is incredible. She just doesn't have 'it'.***

"It's not just sex appeal, it's this thing of using the face and the eyes to make people melt."

It might be diplomatic to mitigate any "off" remarks with assertions that this was just their opinion, and what do they know anyway, but it doesn't make the winners that interesting to us the viewer. It doesn't make us melt. You don't have to be a vile toad who snidely says that everyone else is a pile of poo, just show that you've not had your personality media-trained out of you. You have a right to be there, so don't just hum and grin and agree with every little thing. You can still be nice and come across as a rightful winner, just give the viewer something back.

⭐ For example, you could mention that you fancy Cheryl Cole. It's not like people won't see your point or that the rest of the UK isn't besotted with her anyway, so just drop that into conversation. Warning, the publishers of this book take no responsibility if your nearest and dearest gets in a huff over this.

Baby-faced Eoghan Quigg followed suit and told *The Mirror* he found both female judges a bit tasty despite being half their ages.

Eoghan said: *"I think Cheryl is absolutely gorgeous.*

"And Dannii is gorgeous for her age. Not that the age difference would matter if one of them asked me on a date!

"It would probably be Cheryl for me because she is a natural woman. She would look nice even without make-up. But Cheryl's married and Dannii has a boyfriend."

And cute-faced blubber Austin Drage had the right idea when he blabbed about enjoying being on stage with a gaggle of gorgeous girls during disco week.

Austin said at his press conference: *"Who wouldn't be happy with those six or seven lovely dancers?*

"I had a crush on them – they're all beautiful. I had girls galore on stage.

"My girlfriend was cool with that though. You can be in a relationship with someone and see someone down the street and think they're great looking, it's not a crime."

That way, the press are happy because they have a funny line to run with, the fans who aren't deeply in love with you will hopefully find it funny, and you haven't said anything too controversial that will come back to bite you on the backside. Cheryl said similar things all the time during series five. *"Oh my God, you're gorgeous,"* she purred at 2008 auditionee Joseph Chukukere. *"You're the best-looking girl group we've seen this competition,"* she simpered to 2008 girl group Bad Lashes. Just show a weency bit of your sparkling personality and all being well, you'll be quids in.

If you're a little bit left of *The X Factor*, then adopt the political middle ground but at the same time show how down with Joe Public you are. Nod to commonplace hot potatoes – mention your school if you went to comprehensive school but keep schtum if you went to a posh private place. Or at least say you had a scholarship – preferably because of your outstanding aptitude for singing – or that it was a low-ranking public school. You want people to think you deserve the prize more than anyone else – and they might feel that you're too privileged if you start talking about playing croquet with Tarquin and therefore might feel that you haven't struggled enough to deserve the winner's title.

★ Say how your parents scraped together for music lessons and how you went to extra after-school singing tuition. Juggling extra jobs to fund music hobbies always goes down well on the show. If a little runt in your close family has had their appendix out recently, mention how well they were treated in your local hospital by the wonderful but underpaid staff. You might as well mention that you're doing a sponsored 5k run to buy new sofas for the hospital here too.

★ Get the Kirstie Allsopps of the world behind you and say you're worried you'll never get on the housing ladder and that your loved ones will lose their jobs in the recession. But be careful to steer clear of any meaty topics that divide voters along definite political lines, as, worthy though your opinions might be, you don't want to end up end up alienating the voters who don't agree with you.

★ Mention charities that you support or who have helped your loved ones along the way if you are rather privileged – or even if you're not. How caring of you as an *X Factor* poppet to mention the good work of those charities. How very kind you'll seem if you refer to the pounds you've raised in rattling tins outside of Sainsbury's for victims of famine.

Eoghan Quigg warmed the hearts of kind grannies up and down the country when he told *The Mirror:* **"If I won, I'd give some money to a couple of charities from where I come from. The Dry Arch Children's Centre in Dungiven helps families from poorer backgrounds and The Thrift Shop sends clothes out to Africa."** Textbook.

What's that? Did someone say that your dress is really pretty? Reach around for the label in the garm and prove that it's from Primark (even if you've sewn the Primark label over the top of the Prada one this morning).

"What this old thing? It's dead cheap. Six squids from Primark. I'm a high street chick, me."

(*Note of caution: it might be worth mentioning higher end labels after you've left the show on the off chance that they'll send you a sample to wear when the paps are prowling.*)

★ Be seen at a movie premiere for a middle-of-the-road romantic comedy during the week leading up to the live showdown. Once there, grab one of the stars of the film – or even just anyone remotely famous – and look overwhelmed to be meeting them. Get their autograph and then show it off during your camera pieces and mention how over the moon you were when they said they'd been voting for you. Perhaps call a loved one and squeal down the phone about how "uh-may-zing" it was when you bumped into Lorraine Kelly and she – she off the telly! – knew who you – *you!* – were.

★ Perhaps mention how "humble" your "waste not want not" background was, and contrast it with the luxury of *The X Factor* HQ and all the food on offer: "Look at all this grub in the fridge. Houmous? Houmous? In my day we were lucky to have dripping on our bread let alone fancy chickpeas. Tsk." Another good way of looking all humble like is to be seen on camera running through all of the rooms, arms spread out as if you've just done the London Marathon in three hours and 50 minutes, eyes wide open in delighted shock at all the luxury. You might want to do a run up and then jump on one of the oversized beds and have a pillow fight with another contestant – though be sure not to mess up your carefully mussed-up barnet.

If you're seen as too humourless – like the much-maligned Rhydian in 2008 – it might be wise to be shown on camera doing something "hilarious" like bringing your washing home for your parents to do. What a card everyone will think you are; a proper person off the telly who still, despite being off the telly, gets their dear old mum to do their smalls. Ho ho. Ho ruddy ho.

★ Have a sibling tease you to show what a good sense of humour you have despite being a bit of an old bore. Have a chat with them in front of your parents and family and allow them to mention that you used to dress up in your nan's shoes and put her rollers in your hair, if you're male, or, if not, mention if your family gave you a funny nickname. That way, you can claim to be a great laugh and at least a bit of gentle rib-poking will break up the tearjerkers on the show.

If you can't be interesting, be as effervescently bubbly as you can be. Alexandra Burke came across as a nice girl who was practically fizzing over with excitement at the thought that she'd get to wear designer heels for the live showdown. It might not be outrageous, but at least she sounded as if she was good fun to hang around.

So, two final points to remember in regard to how you come across:

★ If you're really dull or really "wacky" and the public aren't warming to you, you might want to mention a poorly relative who is getting so much happiness from you being on telly. If not poorly, a better looking/much younger/much older/much nicer person of your acquaintance might do. That way, even if you are an irritating oik, people might want to keep you in to save the feelings of your saintly relation.

★ All the accumulated data points to the wisdom of a non-controversial stance on virtually everything with occasional jokes thrown in for good measure, coupled with heartfelt concern for unlucky victims of random misfortune.

No one's going to argue with that.

HOW TO WIN X FACTOR

chapter thirteen

BEING THE UNDERDOG

"May they provide hope for the masses."

Forget the British bulldog. The symbol of this fine land should be the British underdog given how many weakest links seem to capture our hearts. Such is our love of the loser that we can scarcely get through a single reality TV contest without cheering on the clumsy or least likely to scoop the prize.

With shrewd tactics, the underdog can triumph on *The X Factor*. Take eventual *Pop Idol* winner Will Young. Not only did he feud with Simon Cowell on a week-to-week basis, but he was a politics – politics – student who was up against a stuttering teen who looked likely to boot Cliff Richard off his pop pillar as the nation's favourite squeaky clean singer.

In the midst of the dull (Leon Jackson) or sometimes odd (Rhydian), 2007's wonderfully unlikely Same Difference – initially dubbed "two of the most annoying people I've ever met" by a flabbergasted Simon – blossomed, despite their unusual act. Ridiculed and shot down by Louis week after week, they were saved by Simon who had a remarkable change of mind and became their mentor. And, as the weeks went on, support came flooding in for the pair, who somehow managed to crawl into the nation's heart.

Viewers came to love their little voting symbols – including clasping their hands like phones and putting them to their ears – and mimes of "vote for us". Their bubblegum pop performance of 'Breaking Free' from the equally wholesome *High School Musical* was applauded the length and breadth of the country. So what if they were brother and sister? So what if they held each other's glances just a little bit too long? So what if it was impossible for them to finish a sentence without an exclamation-marked phrase! They were our happy Same Difference, whom no one else – or so we thought – liked, and so it was our duty to support them.

They said they wanted to *"create a Same Difference world where everybody is happy".* Publicly, we ridiculed them. Privately, we were rooting for them. Who wouldn't want universal happiness? They might have been novelty but they were refreshingly bubbly, uncool and non-weepy – Sarah's bullying memories aside – and made Saturday nights fun. It took a while for them to be accepted, but their sheer resilience helped them bound their way to being runners-up on series four, striking a home run for underdogs everywhere.

Similarly, the nation came to embrace Rhydian and his operatics. Yes, he had a music degree and preferred Lloyd-Webber to Whitney. Yes, he gave Sharon and Dannii a rose during his audition. Yes, his hair was blindingly yellow. But so what? He was our opera-warbling, bleached blond Welsh Rhydian. That he was a bit misguided or mis-edited or whatever was immaterial. We liked him (and continued to do so: his 2008 debut album went platinum).

If you asked anyone in the final week who they wanted to win, it was a toss-up between Same Difference and Rhydian. Suddenly, pleasant but plodding Scotsman Leon Jackson was in the unenviable position of being pitted against underdogs who looked on their way to being top dogs.

Leon took the prize home, but his shower of tears wasn't worth a millionth of the shocked looks on Same Difference's faces when they realised they had made it to the final. Their Cheshire Cat grins and "oh my God" exchanges were priceless. For many, they walked away the real winners.

And let's not forget quintessential quirkmeister Chico Slimani. So disgusted was Simon by his audition that the sneering one trotted out of his audition in a monstrous huff, convinced Chico would bring down the rightful pop world order. As it turned out, Chico remained in the competition to become one of the most memorable contestants in the show's history.

"Underdog stories on the show have universal appeal," says Scott Allison, professor of psychology at the University of Richmond, *"and are attractive to us because they represent hope, promise and potential. We can all identify with an underdog on* The X Factor *much more than we can identify with smashing successes.*

"These stories nourish our aspirations to overcome the imposed limitations of underdog status. These heroic accomplishments of underdogs may serve as an inspiration as well as a guide for socially sanctioned behaviours. They may also provide hope to the masses who aspire to successfully overcome the obstacles present in their own lives and may suggest that the world can be a fair place in which all individuals have the potential to succeed."

Indeed. Same Difference wrenched themselves through the auditions, remaining bubbly pop optimists despite sneering smears from Louis. It was hard to begrudge them their success, and to not feel proud that they had done so well.

Similarly, the angrier the judges became about pool cleaner turned singer Daniel Evans staying in series five, the more protective of him we felt. They might have verbally bashed him – calling him a "karaoke singer", a Ricky Gervais lookalike and just plain cheesy – but he took it all in his stride and won the backing of BBC Radio 1 presenter Chris Moyles.

The gobby DJ threw his considerable weight behind Daniel and egged on listeners to vote for him – largely to aggravate the judges, who were exasperated at Daniel's success, They, in turn, seemed unable to grasp that the crooning dad came across as A Very Nice Person who seemed to enjoy being on the programme.

"Daniel looks like Rick Astley's dad and has no chance of winning," cackled Moyles, *"and that's why we all have to vote for him! The people at X Factor will hate us doing this. It's going to be brilliant."*

So what is it about the *X Factor* underdog that is so appealing to us back home?

"These underdog stories are powerful," says Scott Allison, *"because, without exception, all of us have experienced struggle – and have been small and powerless early in life and when first enrolled in schools, jobs and social organisations. Therefore, it may be relatively easy for us to take the perspective of those who are also struggling or competing against formidable odds."*

It's probably a good idea, therefore, to play up your underdog status if you are a "novelty" or unusual act so that people feel sympathetic towards the struggle you went through to get through the auditions, because we'll want to feel sorry for you and vote to keep you in.

"Our love for underdogs reveals two essential elements of our humanity," continues Scott, *"one, our keen awareness of human frailty and struggle, and two, our desire to overcome the most difficult of obstacles.*

"Put together, these two elements make rooting for an underdog such an appealing activity," continues Scott. *"Witnessing someone triumph over adversity is inspiring, motivating, powerful and revered. The successful underdog makes the struggle of carving out a good life for ourselves worthwhile."*

(NB: This principle can work equally well in certain circumstances once you've become a superduperstar. Having been entertained by Britney and Mariah's very public wig outs, we thanked them by buying their CDs and concert tickets again. Perhaps engineering a breakdown should be a mandatory element of media training, alongside denying that you've ever taken drugs, and reacting graciously when Elton John passes judgement upon you.)

No underdog has yet won *The X Factor*, so there is a definite gap in the market. Helpfully, triumphing over the indifference of the judges to be crowned the winner will give you a ready-made story to trot out in interviews. It's a tidy deal.

Here are a few things to tick off should you wish to become that pioneering underdog.

★ Always follow the strongest contender when you sing, so that people feel sorry for you having to compete with their heart-tugging version of 'I Will Always Love You', dedicated to a lost loved one.

★ Sing something generally regarded as a bit naff but also well known and begrudgingly loved. Look on *Now That's What I Call Music* collections from the

Eighties and pick something on the second half of the album. Hopefully this will make people smile before they go out on a Saturday night and put them in a party mood. (You can pull a more serious song out of the bag later in the competition when people have accepted you.) Look at Same Difference's song choices if you get stuck: Wham!, S Club 7, *High School Musical,* Starship.

★ Be a bit of a dork, cracking bad jokes ("What's orange and in my hand? This invisible carrot. Ho ho"). The other contestants will cease to regard you as serious competition and fail to notice you creeping up on them in popularity.

Stick with your underdog status. Hopefully, it will pay off – and then you can show how much you've triumphed against the damning indifference of the outside world with a rousing rendition of 'Against All Odds', dedicated to those who snubbed you in a previous life. Hoorah.

chapter fourteen

NEVER BE THE "ONE TO BEAT"

"I've said this from the start, but you are the..."

The biggest noose around any *X Factor* contestant's neck is paradoxically linked to one of the biggest compliments that can be paid during the show. Delivered almost always by a smirking Simon Cowell, the words signal a few weeks of hype and relative bliss before an untimely demise. Contestants of a spirited nature might feel that they will be able to cheat the system with a few choice songs and a bit of hoo-ha, but they won't. Oh no, they won't.

Once those words are uttered, the unlucky chosen one might as well hand back their glitzy outfits and newly found fame and quietly head off, troubling not a single soul as they make the lonely trip back home with the ruinous words ringing in their ears.

And what are these terrible words?

"You're the one to beat in this competition." Cue expectant smile from Cowell and an axe smashed right through your *X Factor* dream.

Sure, he might say them a different way. After all, it'd get very mundane for the multi-millionaire to say the same thing each and every year. Could you imagine?

He might say, "I've said this from the start, but you are the one to beat." He might even drop in a "world class" in there for good measure, but the fact remains that as soon as that sentiment is known, the dream is over.

Oh sure it might come from a nice place. Sure, it might sound nice. But make no bones about it, being the one to beat is a death sentence for *X Factor* contestants.

Think of 21-year-old jazz popstrel Laura White. Cowell called her the *"one to beat".* Walsh said she was *"the voice of the competition".* Her betting odds went up. People raved about that masterly northern mademoiselle who was going to wipe the floor with her "competition". Praise was heaped upon her brunette head from all directions. Even her fellow contestants called her the one to beat.

Said Eoghan at the time: *"For me, Laura White is the one to beat. The way she controls her voice is just amazing."*

Sneaky.

Then she was given the heave-ho in week five. Some claimed they couldn't get through to vote for her. Others claimed it was unfair that on the same week Diana Vickers had been given the week off and an immediate pass through to the next round because she was diagnosed with laryngitis.

For all the huffing and puffing over Laura's exit, the point is that seeing someone who everyone predicts to win sail through and win doesn't really make great television. Series three might have just about pulled it off with Leona Lewis scooping the crown that everyone knew she'd get, but where's the fun in that year after year? No fun, that's what. It might be about the singing but it's still an entertainment show and a wee bit of unlawful bootings and surprise lingerers makes the programme compulsive.

Laura told *The Sun*: *"I'm not going to lie, part of me is angry. I had such amazing comments off the judges and all of a sudden they were taken away. It's been hard to take in.*

"Cheryl thinks everyone thought they just didn't need to pick up the phone."

And that's not all, the jazz singer reckoned the burden of being the favourite and performing well week in week out got the better of her.

Laura said: *"The pressure builds up and it can start to affect you. I didn't completely lose confidence – but I worked so, so hard for so many years and I really believed this would be my big break."*

Bearing that in mind, who would want to be the "one to beat" now? Series two contestant, the ever-lovely Maria Lawson, was 66/1 odds to leave the show on the week she was booted.

Maria said: *"There was so much pressure every week to do something good and interesting, but [choosing] something that the judges and people at home would like and things like being labelled as the 'one to beat' can put on extra pressure."*

But Maria found herself shuffled out of the *X Factor* race prematurely in week five – much to the shock of many viewers after the judges decided to keep in the rather weaker Conway Sisters, leading to much booing from the audience.

Later, even Simon Cowell admitted to *The Mirror* he'd made the wrong choice.

Simon said: *"I made the wrong decision. If I'd have had five minutes more to think about it, I would have sent The Conway Sisters home.*

"I acted out of loyalty, but this show is about talent. Maria should have stayed. The Conways don't have a chance of winning this competition."

Cripes, how right he was. So what can future contestants do to avoid being labelled the one to beat?

★ Be a bit rubbish at something that you can work at fixing. Confidence is one that is usually passable, but dancing is another less soul-destroying one. You don't want to be utterly embarrassing but show the public you're just like them; yes, you might know the steps to the 'Macarena' and 'Oops Up Side Your Head', but other than that, it's just a lot of shuffling and looking at the floor. It'll just give you something to work on, much like Diana Vickers in 2008, that isn't enough to put people off you but just shows that you have a minor flaw.

Poor Diana was told off by Louis for not bopping around the stage a bit more and eventually learned a routine for Blondie's 'Call Me' to hush his cries.

Diana later did a few steps to Avril Lavigne's 'Girlfriend' but was still blasted for being a being static, a criticism that Diana's mentor, Cheryl Cole, was quick to argue wasn't a necessary requirement for a singer such as Diana.

★ Elsewhere, if you are the bookies' favourite, it might not hurt to be a little bit hesitant. You don't want to be too nervy, but a little bit helps to show how much you want "this competition" and that you haven't let it all go to your head.

Alexandra Burke was a bag of nerves before going on stage each week despite getting lashings of praise chucked at her.

Alexandra's mentor, Cheryl, said at the time: *"Alexandra's been the bookies' favourite but actually that's added quite a lot of pressure on to her. She's really struggling with her nerves so I'm just trying to contain that at the minute, and just to keep doing what she's been doing.*

"She comes out there every week terrified and sings and dances amazingly, so I'm not as worried as she is."

Austin Drage, who was seen as a dead cert to get into the final three, found himself in the shock position of being in the bottom two in week four. The Essex boy was modest but hit on an important nail those unlucky enough to be the "one to beat" have to consider – that if they ever do find themselves in the bottom two, the judges might feel eager to give them the push to give their own perhaps less-talented acts a better chance of winning.

Austin said: *"I don't know why the public didn't put me through on this occasion.*

"In terms of judges, maybe Louis saw me as a threat.

"I know I'm good at what I do to be in at this stage, but whether I was good or bad enough to go home, I don't know. "

So to refresh, you can be a thoroughly talented contestant, but be wary of being so unbelievably brilliant that the judges and people at home have nothing more to add to you and won't label you as "the one to beat". There's only one way to go once you've reached the top and that's down, so give yourself room to "peak" and gallop past the fallen "dark horses" as the weeks go on.

chapter fifteen

TALK IN CLICHÉS

"I'm living the dream."

Have you given it 100%? Are you on a journey?
Is it at the end of the day? Did you "literally" give
it 110%? Did you nail it? Did you look like a pop star
tonight? Did you make that song your own? Are you
doing this for yourself and if anyone else likes it, well
that's a bonus?

Well you're in good company then, because it seems
nigh on impossible to get through even five minutes of
The X Factor without banalities like this being blurted out
by contestants, judges and anyone else for that matter.

Phillip Hodson says: *"People watching reality TV shows
like to hear clichés because it's easy to grab hold of and
they feel on a level with the contestants.*

*"By using commonly used phrases and clichés,
the contestant is allowing the audience to understand*

them and warm to them more easily. They don't feel patronised and they can understand the contestant's meaning."

Simon Cowell may have allegedly called for clichés to be banned in 2008, but *The X Factor* is overtaking ITV football commentary as the most cliché-ridden vehicle on television, and it works because of it. *"In these uncertain times,"* wrote *The Guardian*'s columnist Charlie Brooker, *"its never-changing, crashingly predictable nature means it represents a reassuring foothold of stability in an otherwise unpredictable world."*

Here are some phrases for you to learn and to look out for.

1) Key phrases to learn off by heart:

"This is my dream. I've wanted this since I was a little girl/boy."
"This means so much."
"I'm living the dream."
"I can't believe this is happening to me."
"I'm so grateful for this experience."
"The whole show has been such a rollercoaster. It's been a journey."
"I want to thank the judges for their comments. I respect their comments but..."
"Thank you to everyone who voted for me – it means so much."
"I never thought I'd get this far."
"This is my big chance. Chances like this don't come along every day."

"We're all one big family, I'll stay in touch with everyone."
"There's only ever one winner, so I've done well to get this far."
"Amazing."

2) Key phrases to watch out for from the judges:

a) Positive
"You've got what it takes to win this competition."
"Do you know what? I like you."
"You made the song your own."
"You're the dark horse of this competition."
"I didn't like it... I loved it."
"You nailed it."
"This competition needs someone like you."
"You're the voice of this competition."
"You're the one to beat."
(NB: This can have negative repercussions though, as it often spells an abrupt end to the contestant's X Factor *journey – see previous chapter.*)
"You owned that stage last night."
"The fact that someone like you can come from our country makes me very proud to be British."
(NB: Be wary if Dannii says this, as she may be trying out "irony" for size.)
"That performance was out of this league."

b) Negative:
"I don't really know who you are."
(To a boring contestant)
"I don't think we've seen the best of you yet."
(Damned with faint praise)

"That was the worst thing I've seen this series."
"It was just all over the place."
"Not for me."
"It was karaoke."
"The song was too big for you."
"It didn't work. Everything screamed cheap/corny/cheesy."
"Give them a chance Simon."

Learn *The X Factor* lexicon and together with your golden voice, you'll be all set for stardom. Then you can graduate to the next level of pop-star cliché, popular examples of which include:

"This new album is our best ever."
"I wouldn't be here without you fans."
"I can't stand photographers following me."
"It's great to be back in (insert city)."
"We split up over musical differences."

And so on.

HOW TO WIN X FACTOR

chapter sixteen

AND FINALLY...

It might help if you have a smidgen of singing talent, but you can't get that from a book.

Good luck!